DISRUPTIVE

DEMOCRACY

SAGE SWIFTS

In 1976 SAGE published a series of short 'university papers', which led to the publication of the QASS series (or the 'little green books' as they became known to researchers). More than 40 years since the release of the first 'little green book', SAGE is delighted to offer a new series of swift, short and topical pieces in the ever-growing digital environment.

SAGE *Swifts* offer authors a new channel for academic research with the freedom to deliver work outside the conventional length of journal articles. The series aims to give authors speedy access to academic audiences through digital first publication, space to explore ideas thoroughly, yet at a length which can be readily digested, and the quality stamp and reassurance of peer-review.

DISRUPTIVE DEMOCRACY

THE CLASH BETWEEN TECHNO-POPULISM AND TECHNO-DEMOCRACY

PETER BLOOM
ALESSANDRO SANCINO

SAGE SWIFTS

⑤SAGE

Los Angeles | London | New Delhi
Singapore | Washington DC | Melbourne

Los Angeles | London | New Delhi
Singapore | Washington DC | Melbourne

SAGE Publications Ltd
1 Oliver's Yard
55 City Road
London EC1Y 1SP

SAGE Publications Inc.
2455 Teller Road
Thousand Oaks, California 91320

SAGE Publications India Pvt Ltd
B 1/I 1 Mohan Cooperative Industrial Area
Mathura Road
New Delhi 110 044

SAGE Publications Asia-Pacific Pte Ltd
3 Church Street
#10-04 Samsung Hub
Singapore 049483

Editor: Natalie Aguilera
Editorial assistant: Eve Williams
Production editor: Martin Fox
Marketing manager: George Kimble
Cover design: Wendy Scott
Typeset by: C&M Digitals (P) Ltd, Chennai, India

Library of Congress Control Number: 2018964959

British Library Cataloguing in Publication data

A catalogue record for this book is available from
the British Library

ISBN 978-1-5264-6435-4
WEB 978-1-5264-6566-5

CONTENTS

INTRODUCTION: DEMOCRACY DISRUPTED

In October 2018 noted scholar Yuval Noah Harari dropped a figurative bombshell. Renowned for his groundbreaking work on technology and the future of humanity, he had become for many a prophet of our coming 'smart' future – for both good and bad. In his bestselling books *Sapiens*, *Homo Deus* and *21 Lessons for the 21st Century* he predicted a coming reality in which new technology may lead humans to seek anew for immortality and fulfilment. Yet on this day his prophetic words were much bleaker. In an article for the widely read US magazine *The Atlantic* he boldly examined in his view 'why technology favors tyranny', declaring that all signs pointed to future tech such as AI, robotic and social media threatening our freedom and democracy rather than expanding and improving them. He proclaims:

> The revolutions in information technology and biotechnology are still in their infancy, and the extent to which they are responsible for the current crisis of liberalism is debatable. Most people in Birmingham, Istanbul, St. Petersburg, and Mumbai are only dimly aware, if they are aware at all, of the rise of AI and its potential impact on their lives. It is undoubtable, however, that the technological revolutions now gathering momentum will in the next few decades confront humankind with the hardest trials it has yet encountered. (Harari, 2018: n.p.)

The recently deceased physicist Stephen Hawking predicted in his last book (*Brief Answers to the Big Questions*, 2018) that the use of genetic editing from wealthy people may create 'superhumans' that could destroy humanity.

Of course, such technological forebodings are neither new nor rare. Indeed there is an entire intellectual history of Luddite philosophy for those who fear and reject technological advancements. This also followed in the wake of a year-long frenzy about the role big data and social media is playing in undermining even the most developed democracies from the 2016 US presidential election to the UK Brexit vote.

As one renowned British commentator has ominously warned, 'Whoever owns this data owns the future' (Cadwalladr, 2017: n.p.). In a world increasingly urbanising, with two-thirds of the world's population living in cities by 2050 (UN-Habitat, 2016), Meijer (2018: 203) warns us that

> the 'games' around data are of crucial importance for the future of cities. The actors in the datapolis try to 'win' these games to dominate the future of cities.

Against this backdrop, the spectre of bots and sophisticated cyber interference by insidious foreign agents is for good reason dominating the popular imagination.

However, it was only recently that technology was viewed more as saviour than destroyer. Digital advances in communication and data collection were going to shrink the world and make our systems more responsive. Envisioned was a connected, smart and participatory society. Social change would happen in real-time – customisable to people's individual needs. Algorithms, the hidden fixers of all our problems, were to be celebrated not feared. It represented a 'new civics for a smart century', where 'putting the needs of people first isn't just a more just way to build cities. It is also a way to craft better technology, and do so faster and more frugally' (Townsend, 2013).

The question then is whether it is us or technology that has gone so wrong. Who is to blame for this rather sudden and tragic shift from optimism to pessimism? It is perhaps tempting to retreat back into a perspective of technological determinism to answer this question. Technology shapes our possibilities, determining our potential and fates. It evokes a Frankenstein-like image of modern humanity – we created a monster! Obviously, so the conventional thinking goes, big data will erode our privacy and give rise to a 21st century Big Brother. Undoubtedly, social media will destroy our actual relationships and promote a civic society of trolling. Looking further ahead – unquestionably, robots will first take our jobs before taking over our very world.

The problem though is that so much of this technological dysfunction is human-produced. There is growing evidence that algorithms are flawed due to human biases reproducing racism, sexism and classism (see for example Andrews, 2018 on the wicked problem of 'governing algorithms and big data'). Likewise, the most invasive aspects of big data are driven by age-old desires for greater power and wealth. The existential threat of 'mass destruction' has evolved into the hi-tech threat of 'math destruction' (O'Neil, 2016). To simply blame technology is to ignore our own social malfunctions to our peril. Indeed, big data represents 'not shareable understandings of the world, but actionable intelligence crafted to serve the imperatives and answer the questions of those who control the databases' (Andrejevic and Gates, 2014: 192).

Attributing all our ills to technology is also quite simply empirically wrong. It is to pretend that science and innovation occur in a cultural and political vacuum. Over half a century of research rejects such a simplistic view. Instead, perspectives such as actor network theory (Latour, 2005) reveal the influential role of social forces in shaping technological research and discoveries.

Hence, if anything it is us that direct and ultimately guide technology and not vice versa. It is more precise to say that technology and society are mutually constitutive – dynamically co-creating each other (Bryson et al., 2016). Such insights though, at the risk of being blasé, are arguably beside the point. The real issue is fundamentally political. Who controls technology and to what ideological, political and material ends? Are we in a tyranny of technology like Yuval Noah Harari says? And what social economic and political changes are necessary to make technology less tyrannical and more truly democratic?

Innovation vs. Disruption

It is increasingly clear that the progress of potential democracy has been largely sacrificed at the altar of its profitable possibilities (e.g. Stiglitz, 2009). However, if you want to take this critique seriously – which most evidence suggests we definitely should – then it must be followed through to its logical conclusion. More precisely, how is technology serving as a dynamic underlying logics for structuring (Giddens, 1984) society and politics? If it is true that society, politics and technology are increasingly intertwined then what precisely does a viable alternative consist of?

A good place to start such an investigation is the cyclical nature of both capitalism and technology. The market is notoriously volatile, constantly shifting between the highest of highs and lowest of lows. Companies rise and fall, succeed and fail. National economies grow and decline, develop and stagnate. This is a circular process – an economic eternal return of the same if you will. Technology, likewise, is dominantly linked with novelty. It seems to follow an analogous route from discovery to adaptation to becoming outdated. This is often portrayed as a curve or a 'life cycle' – though it reflects a similar dynamic (see Beal and Bohlen, 1957). This is further reflected in the way ideas and policies seem to be cyclical in their own popularity (see McCarty et al., 2015).

Significantly, this gestures toward a potentially profound paradox of capitalism, technology and politics alike. It is captured in the old adage that 'the more things change the more things stay the same'. Formally, at stake is the mixing of constantly shifting conditions within a relatively entrenched stable system. Within the economic tradition this is articulated as creative destruction, first proposed by the economist Joseph Schumpeter. He declares the 'process of industrial mutation that incessantly revolutionizes the economic structure from within, incessantly destroying the old one, incessantly creating a new one' (Schumpeter, [1942]1950: 83, quoted in Kirzner, 1999: 7). Here the heroes are the entrepreneurs as drivers of change. They are constantly in a process of destruction and creation, as the name of the concept suggests. These ideas extend to technology and politics as well.

In contrast are critical theories of political economy that explicitly speak to the possibility of systematic transformation. Open Marxism, drawing on the insights of Antonio Gramsci, discuss the existence of an organic crisis that reveals the fundamental contradictions of a present status quo and its associated social, political and economic relations (e.g. Bonefeld et al., 1992;). In this regard:

> [A] crisis occurs. ... This exceptional duration means that uncurable structural contradictions have revealed themselves ... and that, despite this, the political forces which are struggling to conserve and defend the existing structure itself are making efforts to cure them within certain limits, and to overcome them. (Gramsci and Hoare, 1971: 178)

At stake is moving beyond the cycle of more of the same (Roberts, 2011) – simply believing in a different emperor without clothes for the prospect of actually recreating how we work, live and engage with power.

This sounds like a far cry from technology perhaps. Yet it strongly echoes how economists differentiate between technological innovation and technological disruption. Innovation represents, in this regard, the updating and improvement of existing products. Disruption, conversely, is the creation and introduction of a completely new market. Hence,

> The effects of high technology always breaks [sic] the direct comparability by changing the system itself, therefore requiring new measures and new assessments of its productivity ... For example, you can directly compare a manual typewriter with an electric typewriter, but not a typewriter with a word processor. Therein lies the management challenge of high technology. (Zeleny, 2009: 12)

Crucially, advances in computing do not allow us to make better typewriters but rather consumers of personal computers and eventually smartphones.

This difference between innovation and disruption offers a new potentially exciting possibility for conceiving politics generally and contemporary democracies specifically.

To what extent is technology reproducing social relations and to what extent is it causing political disruptions? If politics is at its root the articulation of what is socially possible, how is the political use of technology being used to limit or expand our social horizons? Will democracy reproduce a broken economic and cultural order or will it catalyse and foster a novel system that is simultaneously 'smarter' and more just?

Introducing the Possibility of Disruptive Democracy

It is not clear if and how representative democracy will survive in the 21st century. New 'smart' technologies such as AI, robotics, social media and automation are threatening to fundamentally disrupt our politics, economy and society. Pessimistically, these advances will only exacerbate existing inequalities and injustices linked to corporate globalisation. However, they also hold the positive potential to radically transform our democracies and civic societies, creating ones that are more responsive, egalitarian and accountable. In these turbulent times for governing (Ansell and Trondal, 2017), we are confronted with dramatically opposed futures for conceiving how technology will reshape civic participation as well economic and political governance.

This book introduces perhaps the most profound techno-political struggle of the 21st century, between a progressive 'techno-democracy' and a regressive 'techno-populism'. It highlights the growing strategic use of populism to reinforce an increasingly technologically sophisticated form of corporate rule both economically and politically. Yet it also poses the possibility of a new social order (Magatti, 2017) where such technology can empower human deliberation and agency to change the status quo and potentially create a better and less unequal world. Reflected is the clash of competing modern 'techno-politics' in which the very survival of democracy and progress is at stake.

The book uses critical theories to discuss the relationship between technology, society and politics. Through a critical journey into recent turning-point world events such as the global financial crisis and the rise of populism, it illustrates four social technologies for governing market, society and politics: the Capitalist Technopoly, Techno-Populism, Techno-Democracy and Disruptive Democracy. While they all acknowledge the crisis of the neoliberal capitalistic system, they provide different patterns in terms of socially innovating and/or politically disrupting this system.

The book will critically investigate how different actors and movements are exploiting new technologies and to what ideological and powerful ends. Secondly it will take the bold step of conceiving politics – whether democratic, populist, or authoritarian – as governing technologies defined as sets of discursive and institutional tools for reshaping social relations. Thirdly, it will discuss implications in terms of power, social equality and the role of human agency.

Most importantly, we shed light on the 'techno-politics' behind these four governing technologies. Because, perhaps, the defining struggle of the 21st century is between competing techno-politics rising from the ashes of the capitalist end of history and whether democracy can recapture its revolutionary disruptive for a new age.

THE CLASH OF TECHNO-POLITICS

The end of the Cold War seemed to be signalling the beginning of a new era of peace and prosperity. The fall of the Soviet Union promised the eternal reign of liberal democracy and free markets. Francis Fukyuma proclaimed the 'end of history', where all major political and economic questions were answered now and forever. He declares:

> What we may be witnessing is not just the end of the Cold War, or the passing of a particular period of post-war history, but the end of history as such: that is, the end point of mankind's ideological evolution and the universalization of Western liberal democracy as the final form of human government. (Fukuyama, 1989: 3)

Politically, it seemed that 'Pax Americana' had been declared and appeared to be everlasting. Fast forward less than three decades and it appeared that liberal democracy and market economies were unsustainable. The new saviours were sovranism and nationalist economic policies from those on the right and socialism and social democracy from those on the left. Even financiers like Eric Weinstein, managing director of Thiel Capital, admitted that 'we may need a hybrid model in the future which is paradoxically more capitalistic than our capitalism today and perhaps even more socialistic than our communism of yesteryear' (Illing, 2018: n.p.) How did this occur? How could the end of history end so soon?

Crucial, in this regard, is to further interrogate the political cleavages and the clash of civilisations (Huntington, 1993) emerging at the end of the 20th century. Arising were new struggles between the local and the global (Robertson, 1995), the secular and the fundamentalist. Ben Barber captured this political dynamic in his now classic and still timely work *Jihad vs. McWorld*, observing that

> The tendencies of what I am here calling the forces of Jihad and the forces of McWorld operate with equal strength in opposite directions, the one driven by parochial hatreds, the other by universalizing markets, the one re-creating ancient subnational and ethnic borders from within, the other making national borders porous from without. (Barber, 1992: 53)

This would expand, of course, into the world-spanning and seemingly never-ending War on Terror, initiated after the September 11th attacks. These were significantly infused with technology as much as with military power. Both sides drew indeed on social media to spread their message. Drone surveillance and warfare became the modus operandi for fighting terror. Complex financial digital methods were used to transfer funds by both sides secretly and securely.

Tellingly, despite their obvious and profound differences these implacable 'enemies' shared a number of equally profound political assumptions. Namely, that the point of politics was ideological (or religious) victory achieved through a combination of military, diplomatic and propaganda strategies. That the aim ultimately is world conquest mixed with protecting their own people – whether it be national citizens or fellow religious believers. The 'Jihad' and 'McDonaldisation' of the world, in this sense, relied on a very similar strategic discourse to that which came before them.

Hence, while these competing social and economic forces – however they are phrased: 'global vs. national/local', 'secular vs. fundamentalist', 'democracy vs. terrorism' – are seemingly opposed, they are also to a large extent repeating the same old political myths with simply a new cast of characters.

The War on Terror was a replaying of Cold War realist politics for a new age. It pitted a crusading West – the protector of all things free and good – against an insidious foe who threated its 'very way of life'. Communists had been exchanged for Islamic extremists, the red scare for Islamophobia. And just as before this soaring rhetoric hid a more complex history of past and present exploitation. On the other side of the ideological divide, the extremists tapped into empowering past discourses of anti-imperialism, independence and radical insurgency. While they praised Allah, like so many secular revolutionaries before them, they were dedicated to liberation through a potent mix of guerrilla warfare and subversive propaganda.

Their uses of technology were, therefore, to a certain extent ironically more innovative than disruptive. New methods of waging war, whether through drone attacks or digital attacks, ultimately fell within the well-worn tracks of anti-insurgency combat and winning 'the hearts and minds' of the enemy. The strategic use of humanitarian technology similarly was a clear rerun of the exploitation of 'humanitarian aid' and, even further back, the Peace Corp for at times rather nefarious imperial purposes. And it goes almost without saying that the fear of 'digital Jihadists' is an updated version of the terror engendered by anarchists and Communist 'extremists' of old.

Reflected was the rise of two competing 'techno-civilisations' who drew on technology to protect their perceived 'ways of life' as well as more fundamentally their shared view of politics and power. Techno-civilisations then represent entrenched ways of seeing and being in the world, a common social construction of our realities by which new techniques and technologies help to modernise and revise rather than reboot and reinvent.

This is not to say that the West and its enemies were precisely the same, or that the free market Washington consensus has been completely replaced. Rather, it is to point out that what can at first glance appear to be quite novel, particularly when linked to fresh technological advances, is in fact rather hegemonic, an updating of past ideas with relatively new practices.

The Technology of Hegemony

By now it is well acknowledged by even the most fervent believers in the power of technology that it is inexorably linked to its social context. It is a deeply embedded part of any culture. Every civilisation engages in processes of research and discovery, seeking out new techniques and methods for engaging with their natural and cultural environments. These can have a dramatic social impact. The watermill and the heavy plough transformed medieval feudal society (see Andersen et al., 2016), for instance. However, the direction and scope of this technological discovery heavily depend on cultural and economic conditions. Thus, for instance, classical Rome had discovered steam power but failed to take advantage of it due to its large slave population.

Technology, in turn, can have a diverse civilisational effect. It can either be ultimately negligible, innovative, or disruptive. In the first instance, it has little to no serious impact on existing social, political, or economic relations. By contrast, an innovative technology helps to update and evolve a status quo – it does not transform it but refashions it and resolves key problems that it encounters in its development and daily operation. Conversely, a disruptive technology is one that directly challenges and transforms a dominant social order.

Significantly, the same or similar technologies can be negligible, innovative, or disruptive depending on how they are used and by whom. Thus mobile phone capabilities can be exploited by employers and governments to monitor and control populations or they can be drawn upon by marginalised and oppressed people to hold those in power to account (Keane, 2011).

Enriching these practical insights are critical theories describing advances in organisation and governance as 'social technologies'. This perspective was influenced by the ideas of the 20th century French thinker Michel Foucault. He proposes power as productive rather than simply repressive – producing certain types of actions, beliefs, and social relations. Power, in turn, is supported by the development of a range of social technologies. To this end,

> Social technology transforms social expertise for a purpose, develops ideas for the solutions for social problems. Thus, it also establishes itself as a part of modern government, it can impact governmental decisions, it allows for a 'technisation', an introduction of new techniques and new procedures, new administrative ways of politics and for a specific conception of power between authority and subject. (Leibetseder, 2011: 14)

Understandably, the focus has been on the role of these social technologies as a force for domination. It refers specifically to the complex and everyday promotion of specific types of governing discourses and regimes. In the words of Foucault, they act as a

> mean(s) to apply economy, to set up an economy at the level of the entire state, which means exercising towards its inhabitants, and the wealth and behaviour of each and all, a form of surveillance and control as attentive as that of the head of a family over his household and his goods. (Foucault, 1991: 92)

However, it is just as pertinent, if not even more urgent, to critically inquire into how such social technologies can produce profound political and economic transformations. Notions of discursive hegemony popularised by Ernesto Laclau and Chantal Mouffe (1986) are particularly useful for this purpose. They define hegemony as the capacity of a discourse – a dominant set of beliefs and associated actions – to shape an existing social order, though importantly never completely so. Quoting Howarth (2000: 102), it is an effort to 'weave together different strands of discourse in an effort to dominate or structure a field of meaning, thus fixing the identities of objects and practices in a particular way'.

The social is hence formed in the continual battle for hegemony. A hegemonic discourse is constantly seeking to define and overdetermine all social relations. Hence,

> Hegemony involves competition between different political forces to get maximum support for, or identification with, their definition of 'floating signifiers', such as 'freedom' and 'equality' (terms which can assume different meanings, depending on whether they are 'articulated' in, for example liberal or socialist discourse), or 'empty signifiers', such as 'order' or even 'democracy' (terms which can be invested with a variety of meanings because they have no inherent content and can serve to unite disparate movements). (Townshend, 2004: 271)

To do so, it creates an appealing vision of 'social wholeness'. Consequently, marketisation depends upon utopian promises of a free world where the pursuit of profit leads to both individual fulfilment and shared prosperity. In his later work, Laclau would refer to this as a state of 'failed transcendence' or 'failed totality', where a hegemonic discourse is supported by a shared vision of personal and collective harmony. He argues,

> What we have ultimately is a failed totality, a place of irretrievable fullness. The totality is an object that is both impossible and necessary. Impossible because the tension between equivalence and difference is ultimately insurmountable; necessary because without some kind of closure, however precarious it may be, there would be no signification and no identity. (Laclau, 2007: 70)

Yet this totalistic domination is always finally unachievable in practice – an impossibility that opens the space for ideological challenges. These counter-hegemonic discourses are referred to as 'antagonisms' which constantly threaten to subvert and replace a status quo. Returning to Laclau's (1996) work, he describes hegemony as forming a social imaginary which largely limits social possibility within its horizon of meaning. The ability of antagonisms to challenge this imaginary catalyses a new battle by contending myths for hegemony.

This continual struggle for winning and maintaining hegemony depends on the creation and exploitation of social technologies. The social is paradoxically both eternally ordered and dynamic. More precisely, the establishment of order, its very stability and survival, is premised on its capacity to adapt and change. Technologies and social technologies are crucial for this process. Importantly, they can be either socially innovative or politically disruptive in their aim and effect.

Socially Innovative vs. Politically Disruptive Technologies

Technology is popularly viewed as a force for change. It is therefore counter-intuitive for many to consider technology as a tool for reinforcing a status quo. This parallels a current irony afflicting democracy. As a political ideal and in practice democracy is fundamentally about challenging and replacing power, a systematic safeguard against tyranny. It is thus not so clear what is the current role and relationship between technology and democracy in terms of their capacity to reinforce and/or challenge existing power relations and ideologies.

We focus here on the issue of whether technologies are innovative or disruptive. This distinction echoes the difference between the social and the political within critical theory (see in particular Marchart, 2007). The former focuses on establishing and maintaining an existing order. It is fundamentally a process of domination. One of the first and still best descriptions of this socialisation is from Karl Marx:

> In the social production of their existence, men inevitably enter into definite relations, which are independent of their will, namely [the] relations of production appropriate to a given stage in the development of their material forces of production. The totality of these relations of production constitutes the economic structure of society, the real foundation, on which arises a legal and political superstructure, and to which correspond definite forms of social consciousness. The mode of production of material life conditions the general process of social, political, and intellectual life. It is not the consciousness of men that determines their existence, but their social existence that determines their consciousness. (Marx, 1977)

The political, by contrast, is the unsettling order that challenges assumed, practices, and regimes of power. Quoting once again from Gramsci and Hoare (1971: 168):

An appropriate political initiative is always necessary to liberate the economic thrust from the dead weight of traditional policies (and ideas) – i.e. to change the political direction of certain forces which have to be absorbed if a new homogenous political–economic historic bloc, without internal contradictions, is to be successfully formed.

It is dangerous though tempting to view these as mutually exclusive, to establish a strict separation between the social and the political. Indeed, even within the most revolutionary moment there are entrenched cultural, historical and organisational features. The French philosopher Alain Badiou (Badiou and Feltham, 1987) offers a compelling perspective to reconsider this relationship. He proposes the notion of the event that introduces new guiding truths for the structuring of the subject and the social. The classic and perhaps most famous example of a Badiou-type event would be the Copernican Revolution. This new truth that the Earth revolves around the Sun completely reconfigured the very basis of the social as such. It provided not only radical new truths to believe it but also an entirely new framework for exploring and legitimising what counts as truth – namely scientific method and science generally.

Within this new 'situation' there are obviously socialising and political forces. Politics stands as a technique for enacting change within this broader 'field of meaning' to borrow another phrase from Laclau and Mouffe. These truths quite literally become the basis for our shared reality – it is the common sense that binds us together and provides a sense of ontological security as individuals. The recent theory of social and political logics proposed by Jason Glynos and David Howarth (2008) is especially useful for conceptually understanding this always contextually rich and dynamic relationship. Social logics, as may be surmised from the above analysis, are those discourses and associated practices that stabilise and strengthen an existing hegemony. Political logics, conversely, threaten dominant social orderings. In doing so they challenge prevailing cultural fantasies and as such a seemingly permanent and unalterable 'social reality'. While not explicit, governance acts as the hegemonic fantasies that organise, regulate and mobilise individuals' subjectivities and identities. According to Žižek, it is

the element which holds together a given community that cannot be reduced to the point of symbolic identification: the bonds linking together its

members always implies [sic] a shared relationship to the Thing, toward enjoy-
ment incarnated. ... If we are asked how we can recognise the presence of this
Thing, the only consistent answer is that the Thing is present in that elusive
entity called our 'way of life.' (Žižek, 1993: 201)

Technologies play a prominent role in this continuous process of hegemony. They represent the physical and cultural techniques and capabilities
necessary for advancing and updating a social order. Interestingly, Laclau
and Mouffe early on in their theories recognise the opposing but always
inexorable relation between contingency with necessity. Yet it is misleading to exclusively link contingency with the political and therefore
disruptive and necessity with the social and therefore merely innovative.
Rather, contingency is an ever-present force that requires eternal nego-
tiation and management. That which is considered 'socially necessary',
furthermore, always demands the creation of new social technologies and
capabilities. As Foucault observes, a novel social ordering

> must not be seen as a sudden discovery. It is rather a multiplicity of often minor
> processes, of different origin and scattered location, which overlap, repeat,
> or imitate one another, support one another, distinguish themselves from
> one another according to their domain of application, converge and gradu-
> ally produce the blueprint of a general method ... [O]n almost every occasion
> [, however,] they were adopted in response to particular needs. (Foucault and
> Sheridan, 1979: 138)

Significantly, it is the very fact that the social is so contingent that it
requires so much technological innovation. Bloom and Dallyn (2011) thus
speak of the construction of dominant antagonisms within a shared social
imaginary – witnessed, for instance, in the framing of politics and social
relations within the US between 'Hawks and Doves' at the height of the
'War on Terror'. Each of these were innovative responses to the accepted
'necessity' of addressing dangerous extremism.

Returning to the insights of Foucault, he critically discusses the notion of
'operations' as those mechanisms and strategies that allow for a prevailing discourse to continue to run effectively. He describes them as fundamental to the
maintenance and success of different types of social technologies, declaring

> we must understand that there are four major types of these 'technologies,'
> each a matrix of practical reason: (1) technologies of production, which per-
> mit us to produce, transform, or manipulate things; (2) technologies of sign

systems, which permit us to use signs, meanings, symbols, or signification; (3) technologies of power, which determine the conduct of individuals and submit them to certain ends or domination, an objectivizing of the subject; (4) technologies of the self, which permit individuals to effect by their own means or with the help of others a certain number of operations on their own bodies and souls, thoughts, conduct, and way of being, so as to transform themselves in order to attain a certain state of happiness, purity, wisdom, perfection, or immortality. (Foucault et al., 1982: n.p.)

Particularly relevant, in this regard, is the vital role of technologies to refashion and update hegemony so that it can tame contingency and prevent deeper political disruptions. Laclau and Mouffe's (1987) example of a football match is telling. They relate how the very framing and physical cultivation of a piece of land as a 'pitch' is based on its discursive construction as being needed to play football. Further, the rules of the game are established and guide the actions of the players. Nevertheless, within this hegemonic framework of 'the football match' there is much room for experimentation and improvement. Social technologies such as new schemes and stratagems can help to regularly refresh how the game is understood and played. New advances in equipment can result in similarly dramatic changes. Yet neither of these technological developments can be said to be disruptive in that it does not fundamentally alter the use of the objects (e.g. the land, the ball, etc.) or the aims of the game.

These insights obviously intersect with existing and emerging politics. The techniques and technologies used to achieve change (whether it be innovative or disruptive) are a key part of any social ordering – especially so in times of heightened uncertainty over past 'truths' combined with rather dramatic and rapid technological advances.

The Rise of 'Techno-Politics'

A central aim of this book is to broadly reconsider the critical relationship between technologies, society and politics. Conventionally, this relation is understood in one of two general ways. Either technology determines politics or vice-versa. Recent efforts to complicate this relation do much to break down this dichotomy. Nevertheless, they fail to fully account for their dynamic role sustaining and challenging prevailing hegemonic orders. Moreover, they do not fully engage with how in the contemporary era technological advances are profoundly altering the conception and practices of governance (Peters, 2016) along with what is deemed presently socially and politically possible.

For this purpose we are introducing the concept of 'techno-politics'. It refers to the techniques and technologies that shape how individuals and groups seek to take power and enact change within and against a dominant social order. To this end, it can contain both socially innovative and politically disruptive elements. At a general level, this concept of 'techno-politics' interrogates how technologies are expanding or reinforcing existing horizons of possibility. Accordingly, the term 'techno-politics' takes seriously the need to critically investigate how different forms and instances of governance exploit technologies – both scientific and social – and to what socialising and political ends.

These insights build upon a growing literature that directly engages and links ideas of social innovation with governance. Jenson and Harrison (2013: 15) in a report for the European Commission have referred to social innovation as a 'quasi-concept', a 'hybrid, making use of empirical analysis and thereby benefitting from the legitimising aura of the scientific method, but simultaneously characterised by an indeterminate quality that makes it adaptable to a variety of situations and flexible enough to follow the twists and turns of policy, that everyday politics sometimes make necessary'. The Stanford Center for Social Innovation, for example, describes it as 'the process of inventing, securing support for, and implementing novel solutions to social needs and problems' (Phillis et al., 2008: 34). In this respect, it stands ultimately for:

> 'new ideas that work'. This differentiates innovation from improvement, which implies only incremental change; and from creativity and invention, which are vital to innovation but miss out the hard work of implementation and diffusion that makes promising ideas useful. Social innovation refers to new ideas that work in meeting social goals. Defined in this way the term has, potentially, very wide boundaries – from gay partnerships to new ways of using mobile phone texting, and from new lifestyles to new products and services. We have also suggested a somewhat narrower definition: 'innovative activities and services that are motivated by the goal of meeting a social need and that are predominantly developed and diffused through organisations whose primary purposes are social.' This differentiates social innovation from business innovations which are generally motivated by profit maximisation and diffused through organisations that are primarily motivated by profit maximisation. (Mulgan et al., 2007: 8)

Yet what is often unexplored is the paradoxical role these new ideas may have for not only improving but also updating and thus preserving a status quo (Teasdale, 2012). New technologies can often mix with these novel ways of thinking for this ironic purpose. The political occurs, hence, when these changes go beyond the innovative and seek a more fundamental systematic transformation.

The prospect of such disruptive 'techno-politics' is particularly important during times of social and economic uncertainty and crisis, where once-sacred truths have been substantially questioned and people are searching for new ideas. The previously discussed Marxist philosopher Antonio Gramsci refers to these periods as the 'interregnum' – a middle period between hegemonies. In these eras, technologies are particularly likely to be politically disruptive. This is perhaps particularly so in our contemporary moment where technology is so heavily associated with technological discovery. Witnessed, in the wake of the 2008 financial crash and great recession, is the growing use of cutting-edge technology like ICTs for challenging the status quo and its dominant understandings. Past hegemonies associated with neoliberalism are being dislocated as the inviolable belief in the free market is suddenly crumbling. Technologies such as big data, social media and smart phones are upsetting previous social, economic, political and cultural arrangements. Hence, technology supporting clashing 'techno-politics' has been replaced by competing 'techno-politics'.

2

OUTDATED DEMOCRACY: THE FALL OF CAPITALIST TECHNOPOLY

It is perhaps hard to remember in retrospect, as inequality grows, the threat of climate change looms and democracy is increasingly globally under attack, that the free market was originally greeted by many with a sense of profound hope and optimism. In the US, where it in many ways first achieved victory, it came on the back of President Jimmy Carter's declaration in the late 1970s that the US was suffering a 'crisis of confidence that strikes at the very heart and soul and spirit of our national will'. By contrast, Reagan and his free market acolytes were promising a new dawn that celebrated individual freedom and the entrepreneurial spirit. Across the Atlantic the victory of Margaret Thatcher in the UK similarly ushered in a new era of hyper-capitalism throughout much of the European continent. The welfare state gradually transformed from a system meant to shield people from the worst excesses of the market to a perceived tyrannical force linked to a bloated bureaucracy and state (King et al., 1998). The point of this brief history is to remind us that the foundation of the free market revolution was as much affective and emotional as it was rational and evidence-based.

By the beginning of the 21st century the religiosity of this movement was increasingly on display. Despite its claims to objective truth, the ideological basis was becoming ever clear. Indeed, even Nobel Prize winner Joseph Stiglitz famously referred to it as a dangerous form of 'market fundamentalism'. He argued that

> [f]rom a historical point of view, for a quarter of century the prevailing religion of the West has been market fundamentalism. I say it is a religion because it was not based on economic science or historical evidence. (Stiglitz, 2009: 346)

At the heart of this fundamentalism was a compelling cultural fantasy of individual and collective prosperity. To this end, our ontological security is rooted in an ongoing battle between forces of good and evil, representing respectively stabilising and destabilising fantasies. Specific to the free market was a tantalising dream of a meritocratic and personally liberated world opposed by dangerous forces that would seek to empower the state and all those who refused to work for their success. Revealed is a new 'authoritarian fantasy' supporting modern neoliberal capitalism in which

> [t]he traditional assumption that markets will lead to democracy has been transformed into a twenty-first century story of authoritarian progress, where a fiscally self-disciplining state and disciplining international institutions will use their power to ensure that countries around the world develop and prosper. Required is not democracy, deliberation, debate, experimentation or a rethinking of core values. Instead all that is needed is for governments and IFIs to rule populations with a firm and 'responsible' hand'. (Bloom, 2016)

Central to this project and this fantasy was a belief in the saving power of technology. Technological progress was already prominent within the post-war Western imagination. Discovery was linked to human advancement. Belief in mass industrialisation evolved into a fascination with how much humans could possibly technologically achieve and how fast. This modern faith in the human spirit arguably reached its peak in the Space Race and the moon landing. Its nightmarish counterpart were legitimate apocalyptic fears over the threat of nuclear war. Technology was just framed as both the key to our salvation and the deliverer of our extinction. It was a post-war fantasy of technological progress that was made possible and intimately linked to public investment and international cooperation on the one hand and dangerous realpolitik on the other.

The coming of neoliberalism did not immediately appear to usher in a new era of technological progress. If anything it seemed to promote the decidedly non-technological notion of an idealised past captured in the image of the US frontier (see Fisher, 1982) or in the UK good old-fashioned British values promoted under Thatcher. It was an example of what has been referred to as 'Conservative capitalism' in which

> Reagan and Thatcher have assembled a rationale and a series of policies for what I will identify as conservative capitalism. Rather than dealing incrementally within a general consensus on reformist policies, they have reversed the growth

of taxation, shifted resources away from human service programs, resuscitated traditionalist prescriptions for personal behavior, and advanced the apparent substitution of the market for government as the key institution of the society. (Hoover, 1987: 245)

Nevertheless, the free market catalysed a new and different type of technological fantasy – not surprising perhaps given its proud embrace of a hyper-capitalist worldview. It was notably manifested in desires for fresh products as consumerism was transformed into a veritable 'way of life' (Miles, 1998).

It also played on themes of the individual visionary, the great man leader and business executive hero who could single-handedly save humanity through their discoveries (Grint, 2005). There arose a cult from the right around the libertarian and free market ideologies of Ayn Rand, whose protagonist John Galt in her most famous book, *Atlas Shrugged* (1957), was held up as a type of entrepreneur idol and was given such sage advice as 'Run for your life from any man who tells you that money is evil. That sentence is the leper's bell of an approaching looter.' Predictably, the entrepreneur inventors such as Edison and Ford were put forward as prime historical examples of the power of the individual spirit of curiosity combined with a strong sense of business acumen.

Tellingly, the ideologies and everyday practices of the free market were also reinforced through being continually linked in the popular imagination to technological innovation. The introduction of 'trickle down economics' was justified by fresh objective economic modelling and forecasting that was thought to be at the cutting edge of human social understanding. The perception was further supported by the continuous presentation of these models as being computer-driven as they were considered far too complicated and contained far too much information processing for human intellect alone. Rather similarly, the suddenly all-important financial sector was associated with the high-tech imaginary of the neon green digital ticker-tape of the New York Stock Exchange and the bold tech-savvy stockbroker. These contemporary Masters of the Universe combined the individual business pluck of the past with the number-crunching hi-tech sophistication of the future. To paraphrase Gordon Gecko from the movie *Wall Street*, greed is good ... and technology only makes it better.

By the end of the last decade of the 20th century the world had evolved into a technopoly. This concept, introduced by Neil Postman, depicted a society where 'the culture seeks its authorisation in technology, finds its satisfactions in technology, and takes its orders from technology' (2009: 71–2). A covert assault on democracy was critical to this emerging capitalist technology. It tacitly and explicitly promoted the need for strong executive leadership, individual competition and strong managerial rule. Governance was at its best a technical process meant to appease the free market. Technology was directed in the service of this technocratic vision of 'good government' for well-functioning markets delivering high GDP type of growth.

The Era of Responsible Innovation

In a profound historical irony, the predicted global triumph of democracy ended up being not very democratic indeed. In the present era where elections are seemingly increasingly under attack it is perhaps tempting to point to the most obvious examples of modern day autocracy and dictatorship. Notably, demagogue leaders have arisen and become increasingly powerful since the financial crash, creating an easy narrative that despotism and illiberalism are merely the culmination of a chronic economic and social anxiety. Yet such simple though not entirely illegitimate narratives miss the potentially anti-democratic logic running throughout the free market.

While ostensibly about the reduction of government as a minimal State (Rhodes, 1996), actually existing neoliberalism has sought instead the transformation of governments and governance to reflect capitalist values and interests. The state has a new and quite significant role in educating the public to be willing and able free market subjects. As Gilbert (2013: 9) observes, neoliberalism

> advocates a programme of deliberate intervention by government in order to encourage particular types of entrepreneurial, competitive and commercial behaviour in its citizens, ultimately arguing for the management of populations with the aim of cultivating the type of individualistic, competitive, acquisitive and entrepreneurial behaviour which the liberal tradition has historically assumed to be the natural condition of civilised humanity, undistorted by government intervention.

Here past conceptions of democratic citizenship and liberal civic engagement are largely jettisoned. According to Wendy Brown (2016: 17), neoliberal reason, ubiquitous today in statecraft and the workplace, in jurisprudence, education and culture, and a vast range of quotidian activity, is converting the distinctly political character, meaning and operation of democracy's constituent elements into economic ones.

In its place, hence, is a vision of individuals who associated freedom and the possibility of the social with taking personal responsibility for their economic destiny.

Moving beyond the narrow limits of liberal democracy, the reign of the free market was clearly openly hostile to any forms of social or industrial democracy. It certainly launched a full-scale attack on the post-war welfare state. Within the space of two decades, neoliberal politicians worked to dismantle or substantially weaken the basic safety net against the worst excesses of capitalism. Even today one British newspaper commentator opined

> Thatcher rescued us from all that. She broke the power of the unions and gave birth to a brand new era of British entrepreneurism, where individuals were left to profit from the fruits of their labour and ingenuity. (quoted in Beynon, 2014: 214)

This mode of destruction framed the state as the enemy and eschewed any distinction between democratically mandated public accountability and conventional authoritarian rule. The threat came from an 'ill-assorted mix of elitists and special-interest groups who see government as the principal vehicle of social change, who believe that the only thing we have to fear is the people, who must be watched and regulated and superintended from Washington' (quoted in Weiler and Pearce, 1992: 237).

The assault on the welfare state was hence a political lambast against the power of democratic rule and decision-making more generally. The very notion of democratic power was being eroded and framed as illegitimate. The state, whatever its popular credential, was a byword for tyranny and inefficiency. It also promoted an immoral idea of society and community that was counter to human nature. As Margaret Thatcher famously declared:

> there is no such thing as society. There are individual men and women and there are families. And no government can do anything except through people, and people must look after themselves first. It is our duty to look after ourselves and then, also, to look after our neighbours.

This underlying disdain – or at least tacit rejection of mass democracy – infected even so-called liberals of the centre-left. In a landmark 1996 State of the Union address, then US President Bill Clinton declared unequivocally that 'The era of Big Government is over' and that it was imperative to shift 'the emphasis from dependence to empowerment'. Even more damning was the observation of Thatcher with regard to Labour's new Prime Minister, Tony Blair, that 'We forced our opponents to change their minds.'

Tellingly, the claim here is not that democracy is necessarily equivalent to a strong and pastoral state. Rather, it is to highlight that at its very core, neoliberalism sought to retell the history of social democracy from a mass popular challenge to oligarchy via elections and protests to that of the victory of an unaccountable and oppressive bureaucratic governing elite. Consequently,

> [the radicalism of the 1960s] decayed fast. It decayed not because it was groundless, but because it was not grounded. What began as the most radical sounding generation for half a century turned into a random collection of youthful style gurus who thought the revolution was about fashion; sharp toothed entrepreneurs and management consultants who believed revolution meant new ways of selling things; and Thatcherites who believed that freedom meant free markets, not free people. At last it decayed into New Labour, who had no idea of what either revolution or freedom meant, but rather liked the sounds of the words. (Beckett, 2010: ix)

This anti-democratic fervor was even more pronounced as regards industrial democracy. Not surprisingly, unions and collective bargaining were viewed as mere interest groups who held back innovation, profits and progress. Their presence as a force for democratising employment relations and the economy was completely dismissed. Power sharing was a value completely scoffed at in favour of capitalist demands for productivity and competitiveness. For these reasons, neoliberalism is often linked to processes of 'depoliticization' (Flinders and Wood, 2014). To a large degree, and certainly according to the theoretical terms we have drawn upon and introduced in this book, the age of the 'free market' has undoubtedly been one where the potential for political disruption of even small-scale political change has been considerably lessened. Political change has thus been managerialised, both at micro-level by letting managers manage and shifting politics away, and at macro-level by New Public Management type of reforms being exported to the developing countries (Ferlie et al., 1996).

Significantly, this ideological move away from democracy catalysed, in turn, a lessening of individuals' and groups' practical democratic power. In his classic work *Labour and Monopoly Capital*, Harry Braverman directly links the growth of industrial capitalism processes of economic degradation and deskilling. Speaking of his own experiences as a worker he observes

> I had the opportunity of seeing firsthand, during those years, not only the transformation of industrial processes but the manner in which these processes are reorganized; how the worker, systematically robbed of a craft heritage, is given little or nothing to take its place. (Braverman, 1974: 6)

People themselves become interchangeable human parts of a market-driven production process. Their alienation from the means of production means they lose valuable capabilities to personally produce things. Moreover, gradually degraded was their ability to learn, create and experiment as labourers. Likewise, the practical decaying and democratic culture under neoliberalism led over time to a dramatic democratic deskilling of the masses. Democracy became reduced to regularised but increasingly empty choices between ideologically similar and elite approved candidates. Power-sharing and collective decision-making were stripped of their daily or economic relevance, relegated to a progressively hollowed out political sphere in which an ever-narrower set of ideological choices and policies was fought over with an ever-higher degree of passionate partisanship.

As Noam Chomsky (1998: 43) cynically but aptly notes, 'the smart way to keep people passive and obedient is to strictly limit the spectrum of acceptable opinion, but allow very lively debate within that spectrum'. It was simply common sense, in this regard, that democracy was an ineffective substitute for corporate rule. In a profound historical irony it was the maintenance of democracy, at least formally, that permitted such a thoroughgoing elimination of it socially and economically in practice.

Yet such democratic deskilling also fostered new and more developed capitalist economic capabilities. Foucault describes this interlocking aspects of power – specifically what he terms the paradoxically mutually reinforcing relation between 'the economic' and 'the political'. He writes that

> discipline increases the force of the body (in economic terms of utility) and diminishes these same forces (in political terms of obedience). In short, it dissociates power from the body; on the one hand, it turns it into an 'aptitude', a 'capacity', which it seeks to increase; on the other hand, it reverses the course

of the energy, the power that might result from it, and turns it into a relation of strict subjection. If economic exploitation separates the force and the product of labour, let us say that disciplinary coercion establishes in the body the constricting link between an increased aptitude and an increased domination. (Foucault, 1979: 138)

Hence, ironically obtaining marketable skills becomes the key to professional success and personal fulfilment.

Technological advancements played a crucial part in this marketisation of agency. Digital advances gaining traction at the turn of the 21st century made finding a job a 'hi-tech' exercise. Castells (1997) spoke prophetically about the rise of a 'network' society in which

[a]long with the technological revolution, the transformation of capitalism and the demise of statism we have experienced in the past 25 years, the widespread surge of power expressions of collective identity that challenge globalization and cosmopolitanism on behalf of cultural singularity and people's control over their lives and environment. (1997: 2)

What he could not perhaps have imagined is just how literally accurate he would end up being. The decrease in democratic agency and skills led to an increase in individual market capabilities – an expansion of one's economic abilities within a much narrower political culture As Flinders (2015) highlights, 'the dominant political culture is no longer one in which individuals either trust or join political institutions'. Levels of political literacy and political trust seems to have fallen among large parts of society and the civic culture seems to have become 'anti-political' or 'post-political'.

Fresh technologies, especially those linked to ICTs, were supposed to help people develop, promote and capitalise on their 'skills'. Emerging was a culture of a technologically 'innovative' market subject. What was reflected was a novel disciplining discourse for shaping and reconfiguring the purpose and responsibility of the government. Theories abound of course about the role of the state in the survival and reproduction of capitalism. Such demands to coordinate capitalism and conform to its ideologies are readily apparent within the contemporary context of neoliberalism. According to noted Marxist scholar David Harvey (2005: 2),

The role of the state is to create and preserve an institutional framework appropriate to such practices. The state has to guarantee, for example, the quality and integrity of money. It must also set up those military, defence, police and legal structures and functions required to secure private property rights and to guarantee, by force if need be, the proper functioning of markets.

It is perhaps not surprising that corporate globalisation soon began to focus on fostering 'good governance'. The goal was to ensure that states worked diligently to change their institutions and activities to create 'business friendly' environments. Significantly,

> [f]rom the early 1990s onwards, the call for less state has gradually been substituted by a call for a better state. This new approach should not be confused with a plea for a return to the strong (Keynesian or socialist) state. Rather it implies better and transparent governance of what is left of the state after neoliberal restructuring has been implemented. (Demmers et al., 2004: 2)

This further became a moral governing imperative. Present was an arising moral economic centred on fighting corruption and decreasing irrational popular resistance.

Yet these disciplining political and moral demands for 'good governance' were not merely a matter of conformity. It was also a dynamic call to be creative in these efforts. There was an entrepreneurial spirit in these expectations. States should find new ways to maximise market penetration within their boundaries. Created within very narrow ideological and regulatory boundaries was the managerial state, one where responsibilisation was shifted to governments to promote capitalism.

It is a 'misrecognition' of structural oppression as an opportunity. Drawing on the developing context of Cambodia, Springer (2010: 931) states that

> [a]s disciplinary rationalities, strategies, technologies, and techniques coagulate under neoliberal subjectivation in contemporary Cambodian society through the proliferation of particular discursive formations like good governance, the structural inequalities of capital are increasingly misrecognized. This constitutes symbolic violence, which is wielded precisely inasmuch as one does not perceive it as such.

Interestingly, as the profound social and economic costs of neoliberalism began to reveal themselves, this expectation for innovation was transferred to discovering and implementing novel ways to balance marketisation with economic and social justice. Or more accurately, to use competitive free market tools or government funding for these broader purposes. Brandsen et al. (2014) talk about manufactured civil society in this respect.

These governmental demands for innovation trickled down, of course, also to the individual. The mantra of our neoliberal times is to be entrepreneurial and responsible. Responsible has a double-edged connotation in terms of innovation. One is predominantly economic, to be resourceful, resilient and creative in order to successfully navigate an increasingly competitive and progressive market society. On the other hand, this has evolved into the demands to be 'social entrepreneurs' (Dey and Teasdale, 2015), whether informally in regard to fostering personal wellbeing and an ethical lifestyle or formally by creating environmentally sustainable and economically empowering managers and business owners. Hence, the new aim of employment was to ensure the 'increased physical and mental health of employees', including their 'advanced spiritual growth and enhanced sense of self-worth' (Krahnke et al., 2003: 397). Cederstom and Spicer point to the dark side of such discourses, referring to it as a veritable present-day 'syndrome', observing that

> Today wellness is not just something we choose. It is a moral obligation. We must consider it at every turn of our lives. While we often see it spelled out in advertisements and life-style magazines, this command is also transmitted more insidiously, so that we don't know whether it is imparted from the outside or spontaneously arises within ourselves. This is what we call the wellness command. In addition to identifying the emergence of this wellness command, we want to show how this injunction now works against us. (Cederström and Spicer, 2017: 5)

Revealed was a new era of 'responsible innovation'. It reflected the introduction of a logic of social innovation. The real responsibility of the modern-day capitalist was to continually update the free market so as to ensure its expansion and sustainability (Porter and Kramer, 2011). It bore witness to how simultaneously insatiable and restrictive hyper-capitalist economic and social reproduction really is in practice. It flexibly disciplines people, organisations and governments to conform to its strict free market ideology while acting constantly to refresh and improve upon it.

The Fall of Capitalist Technopoly

This dynamic though ideologically narrow culture of neoliberal innovation reinforced an ascendant capitalist technopoly. While it praised the individual, it empowered experts and government bureaucracies to promote capitalist knowledge and practices. This also extended to the creation of a vibrant technocracy, 'a system of governance in which technically trained experts rule by virtue of their specialized knowledge and position in dominant political and economic institutions' (Meynaud, 1969: 31).

Those who were perceived to understand the secrets of market success were increasingly socially reified. It represented

the widespread belief that a business-style leadership is necessary for solving organisational, social and economic problems. The chief executive officer is put forward as the embodiment of the strong, capable and forward thinking leader who can get things done. The prominence of the CEO therefore is not just economic but ideological. It is the idealisation of the figure who encapsulates capitalist freedom and success; the individual who is able to achieve their goals regardless of what gets in their way. (Bloom and Rhodes, 2018: 43)

Interestingly, this directly intersected with perceptions of technological genius. By the 1990s, the tech CEO was progressively idolised. Figures such as Bill Gates and Steve Jobs were portrayed as social 'visionaries'. Indeed

Just a few decades ago tech entrepreneurs like Microsoft boss Bill Gates and Apple supremo Steve Jobs started to be propounded as possessing the thinking that would push us toward a bright future. Today that same mantle has been passed on to the likes of Facebook's Mark Zuckerberg and Google's Larry Page. (Bloom and Rhodes, 2018: 72)

These reinforced a wider and more pernicious discourse of economic inevitability associated with globalisation and constantly conformed by its technocratic handmaidens (see Bloom, 2016; Deudney and Ikenberry, 2009; Spicer and Fleming, 2007).

This resulted in a demand for people to innovatively cope with this inevitable capitalist change. It was discursively evolved from a structural challenge to a personal opportunity. Hence, the emphasis in the early 1990s onward on reskilling. There was an expectation that people can become entrepreneurs in negotiating this inevitable shift. Their social and economic displacement could not be avoided. Yet providing people with the skills to be creative and resilient in the face of this change certainly could offer them a sense of renewed agency and empowerment.

Nevertheless, this technopoly was already beginning to be questioned by the turn of the 21st century. The election of George W. Bush gestured to a growing 'anti-elitism' among wide swathes of the population. Despite coming from a wealthy background and being the son of a former President, his folksy manner indicated his popular rather than academic and technocratic credentials. The fact that he was also a businessman further fed into this anti-elitist image. He was the 'MBA President' who used this education and experience to be decisive, efficient and when necessary utterly ruthless (Bloom and Rhodes, 2017).

Yet this anti-elitist sentiment soon developed into something much more politically dangerous to the status quo. The failures of the Iraq War exposed not only the literal 'faulty' military intelligence of the government but also the figurative faulty intelligence of political elites overall. Across the world technocracy was progressively out of fashion. The 'Pink Tide' that engulfed much of Central and South America reflected this shift as well as creeping political radicalisation (see especially Reyes, 2012; Yates and Bakker, 2014).

The faith in capitalist technopoly was thus severely weakened. There was a growing disjuncture between the growing excitement surrounding the private use and consumption of technology with the widely accepted failure of politicians to use it for the public good. This weakened foundation would soon lead to a more fundamental existential crisis of market fundamentalism and its once-sacred technocratic leaders.

3

THE RISE OF TECHNO-POPULISM

In September 2008 the capitalist world came close to tumbling down. It witnessed the largest economic crash since the Great Depression nearly a century beforehand. As august banking institutions such as Lehman Brothers fell in the space of days, the spectre of mass unemployment and material scarcity seized the popular imagination. Amidst these profound worries was nevertheless a perverse hope. After decades of being told that 'There is no alternative' to the free market, suddenly everyone was acknowledging the need for something new. Even the staunchest capitalist supporter seemed quickly to sing a new tune and recognise that indeed the times were a-changing.

The financial crisis represented something far greater than merely an unexpected economic downturn. It was a profound existential crisis – reflecting the need for humanity to reconsider its present existence and future destiny anew. In a sense, it forced on societies a fresh choice concerning what they stand for and what they would like to be. To this end,

A crucial question of our time then is whether we can give up our bad faith in the free market. The degree to which individually and collectively we can dramatically reimagine the meaning and practice of freedom. If we no longer accept that capitalism represents the limit of social possibility. Can we wake up from our dogmatic capitalist slumber to embrace and explore new potentialities for our personal and shared existence? (Bloom, 2018: 1)

Of course, those in charge were either unwilling or simply did not desire to make or allow for such a profound existential choice. Phillip Mirowski sums up the emerging ethos nicely in his aptly titled book *Never Let a Serious Crisis Go to Waste: How Neoliberalism Survived the Financial Meltdown*:

> Conjure, if you will, a primal sequence encountered in B-Grade horror films where the celluloid protagonist suffers a terrifying encounter with doom yet on the cusp of disaster abruptly awakes to a different world which initially seems normal but eventually is revealed to be a second nightmare more ghastly than the first. Something like that has become manifest in real life since the onset of the crises which started in 2007. (Mirowski, 2013: 1)

And indeed in the immediate aftermath of the crash from both the right and the official left the emphasis was on 'recovery' not revolution.

This played into a broader crisis narrative built on an ironic nostalgia for a once seemingly guaranteed prosperous future that now appeared lost (Bloom, 2016). Hence, this turning away from the possibility of serious change was linked to a heightened sense of deeper ontological insecurity and a belief that financial capitalism could be resurrected with just a few little tweaks.

There remained though a need to properly explain what happened and create a new post-crisis sense of political community and ideological purpose. In much of the world this took the form of austerity (Pollitt and Bouckaert, 2017). In this respect,

> The present moment is marked by anxieties about society falling apart, and nostalgia for a lost era of social cohesion These anxieties shape the dominant narrative about the causes of the recession – which are seen as resulting not from the excesses of the financial sector but from a profligate welfare system and an overly permissive immigration system, which has given the wrong people access to public services – the unemployed, the disabled, single parents and immigrants. (Forket, 2014: 41)

Here the fault lay with people and government who spent beyond their means. The solution naturally was for everyone, including profligate states, to simply tighten their proverbial belts and spend less. Tellingly, this was framed as a matter of shared national sacrifice, as happened for example in Italy with the Monti Government. This discourse and its associated policies would, of course, have a global impact.

Across the Atlantic in the US there were publicly made efforts to reinvest in the economy and reform capitalism. The US House of Representatives approved a $700 billion bailout for the financial system, reversing course to authorise what may be the most expensive US government intervention in history (Herszenhorn, 2018).

In the impassioned words of Matt Taibbi (2013: n.p.):

> It was all a lie – one of the biggest and most elaborate falsehoods ever sold to the American people. We were told that the taxpayer was stepping in – only temporarily, mind you – to prop up the economy and save the world from financial catastrophe. What we actually ended up doing was the exact opposite: committing American taxpayers to permanent, blind support of an ungovernable, unregulatable, hyperconcentrated new financial system that exacerbates the greed and inequality that caused the crash, and forces Wall Street banks like Goldman Sachs and Citigroup to increase risk rather than reduce it

Despite their subtle and not so subtle differences, conservative and liberal responses produced the same ultimate response. Notably, it was widely questioned 'who is the government, politics, and the economy working for?' Emerging was a distinct popular crisis to both the free market and the status quo.

Updating 'The People' for the New Millennium

Nearly a decade after the financial crash, a new restless political energy was beginning to stir. Old accepted truths about what made a good economy and who was electable were suddenly under severe threat. The free market, once seen as permanent in its existence and unchallengeable in its rightness – was increasingly under attack from ideological sides. The power of the mainstream political class was similarly besieged. Arising was the era of anti-establishment politics (Nineham, 2017).

The conventional account of this anti-establishment upsurge was that it was born out of economic anxiety, social resentment and widespread dissatisfaction with elites. Not surprisingly, this led to widespread prognostication that populism was once again on the rise. According to a 2016 *Time* magazine article

> For more than a generation, the Western elites settled into a consensus on most major issues—from the benefits of free trade and immigration to the need for marriage equality. Their uniformity on these basic questions consigned dissenters to the political fringe—further aggravating the sense of grievance that now threatens the mainstream. (Shuster, 2016: n.p.)

This label was equally applied to all groups challenging the status quo – regardless of whether they were coming from the left wing or the right wing, like in a horseshoe where the extremes tend to converge (the so-called 'horseshoe theory', Faye, 1996). While undoubtedly these movements share certain affinities – particularly an increasingly broad-scale rejection of the status quo – it is misleading to assume that all of them are populist *per se* and there are of course varieties of populism occurring throughout the world (Caiani and Graziano, 2016). The term, hence, is not simply a catchall for any and all bottom-up movements demanding radical change. Rather it denotes (at least within mainstream academic thinking) (1) a pri-oritisation of 'the people', (2) the emergence of a demogogic leader and (3) a desire to overthrow the status quo (Canovan, 1982). It is crucial, therefore, to identify where populism is occurring and what this reflects fun-damentally about contemporary politics. Most obviously, this populism links to a prevailing dissatisfaction with the current order. It encompasses those who claim to have been 'left behind' and those who proclaim themselves to be part of the '99%'. Their anger is indeed a potent disruptive political force.

They critically reflect the later theories of Laclau (2007) in regard to pop-ulism. Building upon and expanding existing understandings of populism, he highlights the important role of 'the people' – especially during times of social crisis and political upheaval – for transforming social relations. Their significance rests in the supposed separation between a given order and 'the people' it is meant to represent and serve. Specifically, he describes what he refers to as a 'populist reason' that revolves around the discursive creation of a 'people' – itself an empty signifier that across contexts binds societies together according to the diverse ways in which it is meaningfully filled. Additionally, he puts forward a radically revised conception of popu-list politics. In particular, he stresses how chronically unfulfilled demands by a status quo foster solidarity amidst otherwise disparate social groupings to forge a shared political identity desiring full-scale change.

In the modern context, 'the people' portrays an entirely new basis for organising social and political relations. At the heart of this new order is the requirement that leaders challenge elites and 'shake things up'. In this respect, it is principally built on an ethics of disruption – one whose ide-ology is ultimately secondary. Crucial, here, is what Laclau describes as a popular 'demand'. It begins as a concrete demand against those in power – fix the bus system, stop crime, reduce poverty – and translates over time into fully fledged calls for total and complete socio-political change. Hence, the popular demand is fundamentally impossible for those in charge to either adequately meet or politically dispense with. It has morphed into a passionate cry for those on the top to be replaced.

As such, populism by definition combines hopefulness to a certain degree with nihilism. On the one hand, it is utterly optimistic that radical change can and must occur. Elites are seen not so much as impeachable social features but easily and rapidly replaceable. It follows an 'us vs. them' mentality. Politically,

> The nihilists have won this election because being 'pragmatic' does not address the large-scale systematic changes that are needed to fight rising inequality. Nevertheless, the impulse of joyful destruction as expressed through Trump – and indeed Brexit – threatens to make an already bad situation much worse. It would take radical moves to shatter institutionalised racism and make progress on climate change, but no one can be expecting those moves to be made by President Trump. (Bloom, 2016)

This underlying spirit is certainly reflected in the current examples of populism. 'The people' has translated into a defence of the beleaguered and 'real majority'. Predictably, this has readily availed itself of cultural, racial and ethnic essentialism. Put differently, the abstract 'people' are in practice bound by perceived commonalities rooted in race and nationality. The new political battle is defining and redefining who 'the people' are and who genuinely is perceived to represent them.

From Popular to Populist Technologies

To briefly review, the defining features of populism are an identification with 'the people' against a perceived entrenched and corrupt elite. This, of course, has strong resonances with concurrent movements for social change that centre upon democracy. However, they differ both in terms of their overall conception of politics and their use of technology for realising these radical political ambitions. Notably, the goal is to win and wield power for and by the people by any technological means necessary.

Tellingly, the roots of this hi-tech populism are found in the linkages of popular will with ongoing technological advances. Social media was meant to allow for a more connected society – literally and figuratively. It gave people direct access to services and supposedly power holders in a way that was both close to instantaneous and personally oriented. It had quite empowering effects, in this respect. Not surprisingly, these technologies gave birth to Internet campaigns aimed at righting widely perceived wrongs. Seemingly demands for cancelled TV shows to be renewed epitomised this tech-driven popular politics. This reflected a broader trend of internet activism (see especially Kahn and Kellner, 2004; Meikle, 2014).

Technology, hence, provided for the popularisation of power (Meijer, 2016). More precisely, it shrunk the distance between leaders and followers (or service providers and customers) as well as between like-minded people themselves. It was thus a vertical and horizontal reconfiguration of politics. In the immediate aftermath of the financial crisis the first new shoots of this soon to blossom techno-populism were beginning to show. The much commented upon Tea Party exemplified this trend (see Skocpol and Williamson, 2016). Though criticised for being funded and secretly driven by the agenda of large corporations, their rhetoric and tactics were revealing. What it reflected specifically are the two key features of this burgeoning techno-populism. Firstly, that 'elites' were seen to be pressurised to serve the needs of the people and secondly, that traditional norms and institutions were viewed as mere temporary inconveniences.

Yet there was a parallel and less perhaps immediately apparent effect of technology ushering in an era of populism. Namely, advances in ICT and big data combined to create a trending culture. What mattered seemingly above all was how many likes one has. Hence, popularity became at once easily quantifiable and dominantly influential. Culture became a truly mass experience, giving voice and access to an increasing number of ordinary people. Suddenly, it appeared that everybody had an opinion and that they were worthy of being heard. Once vaunted tastemakers were gradually being supplemented and to an extent replaced by hidden algorithms and big data that tracked what was 'hot' and what was 'not' in real time.

There was one final technological component to this populist upsurge. It was one that also helps explain why a movement that is so against elites can so readily embrace the market. It is that technology was meant to make things more efficient, breaking down existing barriers to allow people to get what they want whenever they want. Mobile apps made reading directions, ordering food, booking taxis and making appointments as easy as literally tapping a button on a touch screen. Streaming services offered the opportunity to choose your entertainment and consume it on your own schedule. Delays, processes, government regulations – they seemed to be the very antithesis to progress and the antiquated tools of 'special interests'.

These technology infused elements – popular politics, trending culture and the convenience economy – would combine to forge a fresh populist politics updated for the 21st century. It ably mixed these components to produce a novel governing paradigm for the post-crisis era. This popular politics exploited technology to serve 'the people'. It signalled an emerging vision and cultural fantasy of governance and power revolving around 'techno-populism'.

The Rise of 'Techno-Populism'

The recent rise in populism has been fuelled by a growing distrust and anger with elites. Almost by definition populism is anti-elitist. However, in the present conjuncture this has taken on a distinctly technological tinge. In the present age the people is set against a 'smart' class of political, economic, cultural and even scientific experts. It is a popular uprising that is at once anti-technocratic and to an extent anti-technological while being infused and driven by the latest technological breakthroughs.

To this end, it is important to emphasise how much this movement is driven by a hatred of elites and the perceived 'mainstream'. This may be repeating the obvious but it is worth investigating deeper what was underpinning this elite rejection. Notably, traditional explanations of economic anxiety and racial resentment only tell part of the story. It also resulted from a dramatic and widespread perceived failure of modern intelligence. Indeed, those at the top of the cultural and political mainstream were often lauded for their expert credentials (Bloom and Rhodes, 2018).

The free market itself was thought to be based on objective facts that could not be challenged. The financial crisis revealed how utterly hollow this expertise actually was. It led to a wider calling into question of existing knowledge wholesale. Additionally, there was a creeping cynicism infecting popular discourses – whereby everyone and everything was corrupted and driven by their own selfish interests. Hence, the neoliberal idealisation of self-interest evolved into a general distrust of a self-interested elite.

This cynicism was matched by the profound popularisation of knowledge brought about by digitalisation. Crucially, populism relies in part on processes of popularisation in which knowledge and truth are understood to be universally accessible. A prime example is the 19th century farm populist in the US whose Protestant belief that divine wisdom could be gained by all those who read the Bible translated into a secular belief that their own understandings were just as valid as the supposed expertise of the gilded urban industrialists (Hild, 2007).

Analogously, social media has made information almost universally accessible to anyone with modern and mobile technology. While the global digital divide persists, within many countries economic inequality has been matched in intensity by an increasing information equality. This has created a liberating but also dangerous culture where everyone is simultaneously an expert and no experts are to be trusted – the so-called 'post-truth', which was named as word of the year in 2016 by the *Oxford English Dictionary* (Flood, 2016).

Technology has had another significant effect on updating traditional populist politics. Namely, it has produced a discourse of those who have been left behind in a new 'smart' global economy. There is much discussion, in this respect, of the role economic anxiety has played in fuelling contemporary populism. It is though perhaps more accurate to describe it as techno-economic anxiety. Specifically, it is a fear that people are missing out from technology's benefits, that it is serving elite interests and that they are being controlled by a tech-savvy elite. Emerging then is a new political fantasy of techno-populism. It centres upon people being able to take back control of technology, their lives and their society.

It thus reifies and psychologically invests in an idealised figure who can use technology to shape and direct technology for the benefit of the people. It also frames politics and, fundamentally, social existence as a continual struggle to obtain and wield such total control. Revealed is a new affective political economy – one based on the ontological security in being part of 'the people'. This identity entails so much more than being a member of the majority – silent or otherwise. Instead it involves an identification with feeling victimised as part of a forgotten population which is being exploited and ignored by elites. Moreover, it embraces a belief that others are stealing what is rightfully theirs – non-deserving 'non-people' who are taking advantage of the system.

Technology is, hence, the saviour and enemy. It is opposed as a tool of the technocratic experts who use it to rule against 'the people's' interests. By contrast, it is celebrated as a resource to break through these elitist institutions and lies to more directly engage with power and discover the truth. Tellingly the very notion of 'the people' is never completely defined or clear. This echoes Lacan's concept of 'the real' – the fragmented incoherent heart of our actual existence. The construction and embrace of a given social reality is thus an effort to continually cover over our incoherent 'real' selves.

Here, the constant evoking of 'the people' is around trying to establish an essential self, to feel connected and whole in a world in which identity and progress can seem to be increasingly ambiguous and under threat. Techno-populism reflected the rise of fresh desires to take control of technology and society at any cost!

Techno-Populism at Work

Techno-populism is rapidly on the rise. Throughout Europe, Asia and the Americas in particular there has been a global uprising challenging the 'Washington Consensus' and the free-market agenda. At the core of this politics is an ideological engagement and concrete use of smart technology to promote 'the people's interests'.

Crucially uniting these disparate movements is a commitment to recovering power from an existing political and economic technocracy. Elites and special interests are railed against as self-interested and ineffective. On the surface, technology is also an enemy or at least the devious tools of mistrusted elites. However, digging deeper technology is completely intertwined with this populist growth. Populist leaders and activists specifically exploit social media to build its popular network and bypass 'mainstream culture' to forge powerful and direct connections with each other. This has, in turn, produced related but wide-ranging cultural fantasies that paradoxically reinforce political authoritarianism, economic technocracy and social control.

Techno-Populist Rule

While populism is an avowedly 'bottom-up' movement it typically, if not universally, results in a top-down often demagogic form of authoritarian leadership (Fuchs, 2018). The most famous populists conventionally are charismatic strongmen who can singularly represent the anger and needs of the people against an array of entrenched and nefarious elites.

Technology has always played a strong part in the spread and strength-
ening of this popular leadership. Mass media has allowed populist leaders
to speak directly to a vast amount of the population (see Blumler, 2003).
However, this has been dramatically enhanced in the contemporary period.
Populists are now exploiting ICT tools such as Facebook and 'WhatsApp'
to reach a huge popular audience in a way that feels both personal and
subversive. President Trump famously uses Twitter regularly to directly
communicate to his large number of followers, seeing it as an opportunity
to present his views free from any misrepresentation by the mainstream
media. The Five Star Movement, which has now become the biggest political movement in Italy, started from a blog written by Beppe Grillo and was
spread through digital websites and other online tools (an e-democracy
platform called Rosseau) with no territorial offices. President Bolsonaro in
Brazil relied heavily on WhatsApp groups to spread his message as well.

The second aspect of this techno-populist leadership is the explicitly
anti-technocratic rhetoric. The enemy, as has been noted, is above all 'elites' –
both economic and political. Their greatest sin has been not only working
against the popular interest but also being utterly ineffectual in doing so.
Revealed is a certain paradox of the contemporary populist discourse. The
ruling elite are at once considered evil geniuses, trying to sell out the 'real
people' and supposedly completely helpless to get anything done even if they
desired to do so. Notions of technology and power play into both of these
tropes. On the one hand elites are criticised for using technology to exploit
everyday citizens. On the other, they are accused of being technology smart
without also being effective. Revealed is a simultaneous critique of a technological elite and the stifling bureaucratic effects of technocracy overall.

The fantasy of the populist strongmen draws upon and bridges this
seemingly contradictory discourse. It promotes a charismatic 'winner' who
can use technology 'to get things done' on behalf of 'the people'. Returning
to the example of Trump, he continually brags about his being 'the best'
and having the ability to 'make deals' as well as his (largely imagined)
record of unprecedented accomplishments as president. Parroting these
ideas was one of Trump's key advisors, Jared Kushner, who described their
election strategy by stating:

> We ran the campaign like a business. We tried a lot of new things. We weren't
> afraid to make changes. We weren't afraid to fail. I found in politics is people
> build these big, bureaucratic machines designed not to make mistakes and not

to have anyone to blame. We tried to do things very cheaply, very quickly. And if it wasn't going to work, we would kill it quickly. The media would write a quick story saying, 'They don't know what they're doing.' But we were just saying, 'Look, we tried, it didn't work. Move onto the next.' (Bertoni, 2017: n.p.)

Social media is especially conducive to spreading and sustaining such populist rule. Significantly, populism is largely a 'thin' ideology (Mudde, 2013) that 'only speaks to a very small part of a political agenda', while

> An ideology like fascism involves a holistic view of how politics, the economy, and society as a whole should be ordered. Populism doesn't; it calls for kicking out the political establishment, but it doesn't specify what should replace it. So it's usually paired with 'thicker' left- or right-wing ideologies like socialism or nationalism. (Friedman, 2017: n.p.)

For this reason it treads more on passion than a firm belief in an entrenched set of political or ideological principles. This makes it especially suited to the age of digital connections and communications. Quoting from a 2017 Brookings Report:

> Social media is particularly conducive to the emotional appeals embraced by populists. Candidates attract many supporters by responding viscerally to feelings of injustice and anxiety, a political approach readily employed in the wake of terrorist attacks ... Populists consistently experience surges in social media following and engagement after specific news events, especially terrorist attacks. This suggests that populists turn to social media following major national tragedies to identify enemies to the nation and make calls for swift action. Most centrist politicians are wary of doing the same, favoring deliberate messaging that seeks to assuage a frightened nation while upholding multicultural and religious tolerance. Evidently, a populist narrative translates well into short tweets and posts that reinforce the tendencies of some and spark feelings of outrage in others. (Hendrickson and Galston, 2017: n.p.)

Populist Technocracy

Populism is almost universally connected to a rejection of technocracy and technocrats. Indeed the attraction of present populist leaders is precisely their rejection of elite experts and bureaucratic governing institutions. Their popularity rests precisely on their capacity to challenge those at the top in the name of 'the people'. Yet ironically, the contemporary era is witnessing the use of populist rhetoric and ideas to reinforce a technocratic-based neoliberal status quo. In particular, it represents a mass movement rallying behind a charismatic 'rational' leader who can restore order and decency in the face of rising political extremism. Central to this emerging 'rational' politics is the promise that this populist technocracy can use technology to deliver 'reasonable' progress combining free market principles with ostensible desires for social and economic justice.

Absolutely critical, in this regard, is the construction of a new 'rational' populist resistance. The Global Financial Crisis made formerly popular political identities of 'centrism' and 'moderation' suddenly very politically unfashionable to say the least. However, the explosion in populism has created a definite desire for a supposed 'return to political sanity'. Arising thus, is a 'rational people' – a supposed majority who rejected the perceived extremist barbarian hordes on both sides of the ideological divide who are destroying their country and society from the inside out.

Tellingly, these movements have taken on key aspects of the very populist politics they so vehemently reject. The shocking loss of the 2016 Presidential election by Hillary Clinton reinvigorated an anti-Trump 'resistance' that relied heavily on social media for mobilising and connecting its members. While these groups are commonly divided in terms of their underlying ideological commitments, there is a prominent element that has turned Clinton into not only a questionable feminist icon but a bona fide populist hero to many. In 2017, she proclaimed 'I'm now back to being an activist citizen and part of the resistance. ... Activism is more important than ever, and it's working, from the women's marches across the country and around the globe to helping to bring down the Republicans' terrible health care bill. ... But we have to keep going' (Merica, 2017: n.p.).

Importantly, these are not the results of centrist astro-turfing efforts. Rather, they are relatively organic expressions of an enraged 'people' who feel marginalised and left behind by the far right takeover of politics, and who see the moderate part of the Democratic Party as delivering us from these extremist evils. Even more worrying, it fosters a new popular embrace by the centre–left 'majority' for establishment figures and institutions that were once reviled or at the very least morally questioned. This has been referred to as 'Trumpwashing' where

> [n]ot so long ago, the idea of liberals hankering nostalgically for Bush, hanging on Kissinger's words or cheering assertions of American exceptionalism would have been unthinkable. Likewise the idea of rooting for the rightwing attorney

general Jeff Sessions, the former FBI director and registered Republican Robert Mueller, and other mandarins of the so-called 'deep state'. Yet old certainties have been shaken, roles reversed and loyalties scrambled by Trump's profoundly unorthodox presidency. (Smith, 2018)

Thus, in a supreme historical irony, human rights lawyer and professor Dan Kovalik observes that

> liberals have decided that 'the enemy of my enemy is my friend', especially when 'my enemy' is Donald J Trump. And so, bizarrely, liberals have decided that the CIA and FBI – despite their well-known history of suppressing civil liberties and civil rights in this country and abroad – are now noble institutions which should be believed and respected. This is because the CIA and FBI have largely taken an oppositional stance towards Trump. Even George W Bush, who was hated by liberals especially because of the Iraq war (which the CIA helped lie us into, by the way), is now considered a sweet, old grandpa figure who liberals coo over, especially when he is bantering with Michelle Obama. (quoted in Smith, 2018: n.p.)

In this respect, neoliberal technocracy is reinvented as a techno-populist vehicle to ward off the 'irrational' politics of both the right and the left in the name of a more inclusive and 'smart' status quo. The French President, Emmanuel Macron, similarly to Matteo Renzi earlier in Italy, epitomises this type of paradoxical populist politics. On the surface, he exemplifies the free market technocrat graduating from the highly selective Ecole Nationale d'Administration and serving in the Ministry of Economics and Finance as the 'Inspector of Finance' followed by a period where he worked as an investment banker for the Rothschilds. Yet his victory was built on drawing widespread popular support in directly challenging the far right upsurge of Marine Le Pen and the far left popularity of Jean-Luc Mélenchon. His rhetoric was one of representing 'all the French people' and was invigorated by an anti-establishment spirit against the outdated French political class. He claimed, thus, that he was attempting to

> reconciliate memories. ... A fraction of the left constructed a memory connected to class struggles and anticolonialism. ... At the same time, a fraction from the right chose a historical view reduced to an identitarism, with which it builds its relationship with the Republic [to create] a new, fresh politics of the Centre, liberal in economics and social in sensibility. (quoted in Henry, 2017: n.p.)

This effort to unite 'the people' was connected to a fundamental ideological project to transform France into 'a startup nation, meaning both a nation that works with and for the startups, but also a nation that thinks and moves like a startup' (Bock, 2017).

Just as importantly, he alone could break through the establishment and protect the French people against Conservative elites from the top and the irrational masses from below. Once in power, he exploited this populist rhetoric to implement further market oriented reforms. He criticised existing political parties for creating 'barriers ... between politicians and the people'. He further justified his free market 'modernisation' agenda as a populist attack on a supposedly privileged set of protected workers, proclaiming

> On the side of those who benefit from a stable and permanent contract, there are millions of people condemned to perpetual precariousness. .... Our country needs regulations. .... But our current regulations, elaborated at the end of the Second World War, do not correspond any more to today's challenges. They favour insiders, that is to say those who are in employment and more protected than others, on the back of outsiders, that is to say younger people, the less educated and the more fragile. (Macron, 2017: 123)

These sentiments were further infused with a strong contemporary technological component. Specifically, he linked social mobility and progress to the broader 'Uberisation' of the economy. He stated:

> Go to Stains [a suburb north of Paris characterised by high levels of poverty and a concentration of ethnic minorities] and explain to young people who work as drivers for Uber that it is better to stay in their projects or be drug dealers. The neighbourhoods in which Uber hires people are neighbourhoods in which we have nothing to offer them. In fact, they work 60 or 70 hours to make the minimum wage. But they get dignity ..., they wear a suit, a tie ... Did we do anything better in the last 30 years? (quoted in Gedron, 2017)

Revealed in the cases of Clinton and Macron are the ironic possibilities of a reinvigorated techno-populist technocracy. The techno-populist technocracy is well epitomised by the Yellow–Green (Five Star–The League coalition) Italian populist government which has appointed a technocrat as prime minister. The neoliberal order is refreshed as a popular demand for 'smart reforms' that enhance social inclusion while defending the 'rational people' against the entrenched 'unimaginative' elites and the extremism of 'deplorables' on both sides of the ideological spectrum. It views itself as subversive, anti-establishment and technologically sophisticated. In this respect, it is an attempt to bring about a new day for an old politics.

Establishing Techno-Populist Control

Techno-populism is at its core a politically disruptive movement. It is aiming to shake up the status quo, even ironically in the name of saving it via a new techno-populist technocracy. Yet it also offers an updated framework for exerting popular control. Specifically, it advocates the use of innovative technological resources to serve and hold people accountable for their everyday actions and views. It reflects a bottom-up form of disciplining that is equally anti-establishment and oppressive.

Highlighted are wider desires to popularly take back and reassert control over technology and populations. It is witnessed in the efforts to inject a strong dose of techno-populism against reigning technopoly and its discourses of top-down innovation led by experts. Here it is 'the people' exploiting technology and not the other way around. In practice this often means the implementation of invasive and oppressive regimes of both top-down surveillance and bottom-up 'sousveillance' (Mann and Ferenbok, 2013). It is channelled into the transformation of techno-populism into a 'smart' and increasingly totalistic form of popular disciplining and control. The case of the far right populist Philippine President Rodrigo Duterte is instructive, in this respect. Behind his braggadocio lies a regime that combines toxic populist appeal with brutal human rights offences. Indeed,

> [s]ince being elected in May 2016, Duterte has turned Facebook into a weapon. The same Facebook personalities who fought dirty to see Duterte win were brought inside the Malacañang Palace. From there they are methodically taking down opponents, including a prominent senator and human-rights activist who became the target of vicious online attacks and was ultimately jailed on a drug charge. (Etter, 2017: n.p.)

Importantly, while often implemented from the top down, these regimes are often viewed as horizontal in their actual implementation and operation. Returning again to the Philippines, Duterte built this hi-tech oppression on a social media-fuelled popular movement. Notably,

Duterte, a quick social media study despite being 71 at the time of the election, took it from there. He hired strategists who helped him transform his modest online presence, creating an army of Facebook personalities and bloggers worldwide. His large base of followers—enthusiastic and often vicious—was sometimes called the Duterte Die-Hard Supporters, or simply DDS. No one missed the reference to another DDS: Duterte's infamous Davao Death Squad, widely thought to have killed hundreds of people. (Etter, 2017: n.p.)

Likewise, such techno-populist control is commonly used to target 'undesirables' that are deemed a threat to 'the people'. As such, it provides the tools for a rebooted form of vigilante justice where social media and mobile technologies are used to report undesirables. These new techno-populist regimes of control are significantly not limited to exclusively populist governments. They are also infiltrating and transforming how states and corporations in general monitor and discipline their citizens. This is epitomised in China's new 'social credit score', which has been ominously described as 'big data meets Big Brother':

Imagine a world where many of your daily activities were constantly monitored and evaluated: what you buy at the shops and online; where you are at any given time; who your friends are and how you interact with them; how many hours you spend watching content or playing video games; and what bills and taxes you pay (or not) … now imagine a system where all these behaviours are rated as either positive or negative and distilled into a single number, according to rules set by the government. (Botsman, 2017: n.p.)

Yet despite these dystopian visions, many Chinese have embraced it as a means of enacting daily forms of popular control. According to 32-year-old entrepreneur Chen, 'I feel like in the past six months, people's behaviour has gotten better and better. For example, when we drive, now we always stop in front of crosswalks. If you don't stop, you will lose your points. At first, we just worried about losing points, but now we got used to it' (Ma, 2018: n.p.).

At stake is the transformation of populist anger into a tech-driven politics of increasingly total popular control. Everyone is being progressively monitored, judged and disciplined to prove that they are a good member of 'the people'. Enemies are easily identified and targeted for scorn and retribution. The hated status quo is being rapidly replaced with an even stronger and more empowered invasive elite regime.

The Challenges of Techno-Populism

This chapter introduced the concept of 'techno-populism' as a novel technologically enhanced and fuelled politics threatening to engulf countries across the world. It is driven by legitimate economic worries and barely repressed racial and ethnic resentments. Its appeal is precisely in being acknowledged and publicly feted by leaders in a modern global society that they once thought had 'left them behind'. In its place they are willing to revive old hatreds combined with cutting-edge ways to avoid once again being politically marginalised, socially disparate and economically ignored.

While it is tempting to dismiss these feelings, there is a reason they are so inspiring to increasingly so many. It is built above all else on an impassioned spirit of 'hopeful nihilism'. It represents the possibility to tear down a system perceived to be rotten to its very core, regardless of the ultimate social or economic costs. Accordingly, it reflects a disruptive political ethos that despite its ethically troubling aspects and real world consequences is inspiring for many after decades of being told we had reached the proverbial 'end of history'.

Yet there are key challenges holding such techno-populism back from being a contemporary force for progressive change. The first is its rootedness in nostalgia. Its railing against elites is seemingly an end in and of itself. The future that will be created after the popular uprising is much murkier. In its place has arisen a deep seated embrace of a past golden age. This slogan is not just an ominous dog whistle to the country's worst racist, xenophobic, sexist, jingoistic instincts. It also reveals a complete lack of critical imagination toward the future. Thus while techno-populists are certainly hopeful and increasingly tech-savvy, they remain uninspiring as to what a different type of society may look like and could be created. They sustain their commitment to believing in seemingly nothing better than a nostalgic past that was always more fantasy than reality in the first place.

The second challenge is the ability to escape tribalism to actually create a genuine popular resistance to elites. At present 'the people' have become dominantly associated with essentialism ideas around race, geography, culture and nation. Yet populist reason is actually meant to dispel these parochial allegiances. It is instead meant to forge a new identification around shared desires for fundamental systematic change and popular empowerment. It is this price that has always plagued populist movements historically. Without such a political commitment it can easily be exploited to further victimise historically disenfranchised groups and all the while continuing to entrench the power of elites. Finally, while there is a passionate populist faith in 'the people' it has no such belief or seeming concern about the survival of democracy. For this reason, it easily exchanges democratic rights for popular rule, dangerously conflating the constitutional and democratic space (Mudde, 2013).

4

THE GROWTH OF
TECHNO-DEMOCRACY

The 21st century was meant to be the golden age of democracy. Instead, the first decades of the new millennium have witnessed a distinct erosion of the popular faith in democracy (Mounk, 2018; Roberts, 2016). It is now viewed as not only almost irredeemably corrupted by elites and special interests but also as fundamentally ineffectual and irrational.

The constant neoliberal refrain that 'there is no alternative' has, as shown, fundamentally degraded democracy itself. It became an exercise in at best choosing the 'lesser evil' and at worst becoming complicit in reproducing a fatally flawed social and economic order. The belief in the changing power of democracy was decreased, making it appear less as the driving motor of social transformation and more a reordering of the deck-chairs on the sinking capitalist *Titanic*.

As a result people look to other less than fully democratic avenues to challenge the status quo. From the bottom, this could be seen in the resurgence of street protests throughout the late 1990s and early 2000s railing against corporate globalisation (Smith, 2001). Globally, this was witnessed in struggles such as the Peasants land movement in Brazil (Soriano and Nunes, 2017). Yet it also saw the growing belief that truly disruptive social change could only happen from the top down – notably via the genius of 'visionary' entrepreneurs. As discussed previously, the most famous of these are perhaps the likes of Steve Jobs and Bill Gates. They reflected an emerging idolising of the business executives as driving human and social progress. Elon Musk, for instance, boldly claimed that it would be his company – not any technocratic government – that would be responsible for colonising the moon (BBC, 2018). Likewise this is the new age of 'philanthropic executives', those CEOs who cover over their own less than ethical labour, production and taxation practices by giving away their money to good causes (Rhodes and Bloom, 2018). These executives are held up as exemplars of creating change quickly and effectively. Beneath their PR-driven generosity lies a profound and growing crisis of democracy.

Fundamentally, people were losing faith in their ability to transform society. Decision-making increasingly appeared to be in the hands of an unelected elite few (Vibert, 2007). Not surprisingly, perhaps, people turned their attention inward to individual transformation. Just as troubling, for many it seemed that such non-democratic executive rule was a far better alternative than traditional forms of collectivised power and popular decision-making. This crisis was only exacerbated by the rising opportunities and threats posed by emerging technologies.

The Trouble with E-Democracy

Technology is now more and more portrayed as bringing about democracy's doom. From social bots to Internet trolls, the digital enemies of democracy are seemingly everywhere. However, it was not so long ago that technology was meant to save democracy – or at the very least vastly improve it. At the dawn of the new millenium, e-democracy in particular was on the rise (Thomas and Streib, 2005). Digital advances were expected to make, in this respect, public services more efficient and responsive (Howard, 2001), as in the exemplary case of Estonia (Kattel and Mergel, 2018). It painted an inviting almost utopian picture of a hi-tech liberal democratic future.

The reality, of course, was in many contexts much less welcoming. In practice e-democracy suffered from serious technical and political malfunctions. Technologically, its promise of greater efficiency and responsiveness was undermined by continual system breakdowns and costly IT infrastructure projects with some fundamental threats to electronic voting in free elections, as in the case of hackers' attacks on the voter registration databases in Arizona and Illinois before the US 2016 elections or in other cases during elections in Latin America and Ukraine (see Akpan, 2016). Politically, this led to a culture of consultation rather than genuine empowerment participation and decision-making (Cooke and Kohtari, 2001). It further encouraged people to participate in what felt like a rigged system.

Learning, thus, more about the biographies and plans of political elites did not translate into the fostering of a responsive modern democracy system. Logging in is not the same as having genuine democratic power. What is crucial, in this regard, is that this growing digitalisation of culture transformed democracy from being a system built on wielding power and influence into one based largely on greater access to information and, in principle, services. E-Democracy did not make elections more competitive or policy decisions less technocratic and elite-driven, or ideologically expand what was considered politically possible. Rather, in most cases it provided people with increased access to official information and wider forums to voice their displeasure. In essence e-democracy was data-rich and power-poor.

This extended also to the workplace. The late 20th century saw the rapid and sustained decline of industrial democracy, as already discussed. In its place arose employer friendly and quite controlling HR regimes. E-processes did little to stem this tide. Instead it analogously gave people access to information about their processes and contracts with little about how to increase their actual collective and individual power.

E-democracy, hence, represented in many cases the hi-tech hollowing out of real democratic power sharing and accountability, rather than relocating participation within a radical politics of development (Hickey and Mohan, 2005). It reflected, by contrast, the ability of people to know more about the elites who rule them. When participatory systems were experimented with they were subject to fit within quite narrow ideological limits. For example, many diverse experiences of participatory budgeting (Ganuza and Baiocchi, 2018) gave just a limited amount of public money for citizens to decide how to allocate. As such, it contributed in many cases to deepening this general crisis of democracy where it was viewed as both ineffectual at best and utterly co-optive at worst.

It did have one disruptive effect though, it led to a stronger democratisation of entertainment and vice-versa. The Internet served even from its earliest popular incarnations as a place for making politics more lurid and voyeuristic, as for example occurred in the Starr report (CNN, 1998). It fed into the scandal industry, turning politicians into easy fodder for the tabloid press and contributing to the trivialisation of the public debate (Flinders and Wood, 2014). Likewise, where e-democracy really thrived was in the entertainment world. Reality competitions harnessed digital advances to allow viewers to decide winners and losers. Perhaps ironically, the most vibrant democratic culture in terms of participation, passion and demands for accountability seemed to be in popular entertainment not formal politics. Paradoxically, e-democracy helped make real elections mere spectacles and official spectacles more genuinely democratic.

It is then no wonder that people were quickly losing faith in the power of democracy. It gave people voice with little actual possibility of translating it into real action. This democratic deficit reached far into the future as well. Indeed, if democratic institutions and processes couldn't solve present problems, how could it ever be dreamt that democracy might address the more disruptive pressures of tomorrow? It appeared that the future and the spectre of a new tech industrial revolution would have little need or use for democracy.

The Rise of Techno-Democracy

Contemporary democracy suffers from a range of malpractices (e.g. the Cambridge Analytica scandal, trolls, fake news, private money influence) such that the authenticity of its results is in some cases in doubt. In the US officially approved gerrymandering alongside wide-ranging claims of voter suppression of minorities and the poor have done much to discredit the sanctity of democracy in practice. Yet from these rotting foundations, have arisen like a phoenix attempts to technologically and socially reboot democracy.

In the aftermath of the financial crisis, new protest movements emerged against the power of economic elites. The self-proclaimed 'Occupy Movement' publicly contested the role of the '1%' through innovative forms of civic disobedience and community building (Uitermark and Nicholls, 2012). What distinguished it, in part, from similar movements, such as the anti-globalisation protests of the late 1990s, was its innovative use of technology (Costanza-Chock, 2012). It proposed a new type of daily democratic culture that was both people-centred and hi-tech.

This infusion of technology for rebooting 21st century democracy was not consigned to the streets. Instead it formed a common cause with more established forms of electoral politics. While not, of course, ultimately successful, it should be remembered that before condemning the practices of Trump, the Clinton campaign trumpeted their own innovative use of big data. The most notable example though is most certainly Barack Obama's campaign. What made it so historic was not simply that it witnessed not only the election of the first non-white President but also its then ground-breaking use of technology for achieving this landmark result (Miller, 2008).

Coming into clearer view is a new politics of 'techno-democracy'. It is composed of three distinct but interrelated elements. First, it is all together committed to revealing the contingency of the present social order – its utter changeability – as well as the power of democracy to achieve such fundamental change. Secondly, it is linked either explicitly or implicitly with the use of technology to disrupt the present order in the name of a new hi-tech political identity – in this case the 'smart democratic citizen'. Finally, it rests on a governing fantasy in which a corrupt status quo can be held more accountable through the force of democratic protest and norms heavily aided by recent digital and big data advances.

It is worth here quickly comparing and contrasting techno-democracy from techno-populism. Both are similarly focused around the desire to exploit technology to disrupt and replace the power of technocratic elites. They are analogously anti-establishment and each suffers, though in dramatically different ways, the critical propensity to paradoxically ultimately strengthen the very elites they are ostensibly railing against. However, there are also real and profound differences.

Namely, techno-democrats seek to promote the 'democratic' citizen, prioritising the ability of the largest number of people to vote, protest and have their voices heard. They aim to establish not merely popular rule but inclusive democratic governance. Further, their deployment of technology directly targets not just a status quo or set of 'elites' but also the need to keep those in authority in check. Its emphasis is on preserving the rights of the individual and the sanctity of democratic principles. Lastly, its governing fantasy is grounded in its efforts to preserve and perfect democracy rather than an essentialised identity or tribal nationalism. It promises to disrupt a corrupt status quo that perverts democracy for its own elite interest. They are the proclaimed saviours of democracy not the people – a galvanising evangelical mission that is both its progressive strength and at times its most radical tragedy.

Practising 'Techno-Democracy'

Technology has the ability to massively transform and even revolutionise contemporary democracy. It can digitally enlarge what is considered politically possible with both established and new democratic frameworks. It can challenge prevailing democratic elites and expand how democracy is practised and by whom. However, it can also cling to preserving an out-dated system and status quo in the name of protecting democracy against the proclaimed 'deplorable' and 'irrational' masses.

'Techno-Democratic' Renewal

After decades of being told they had been thrown on the 'ash heap of history', the social democratic left is once more on the rise within the left spectrum. Politicians from the avowedly and unashamedly progressive and socialist tradition have emerged in renewed force, putting the political and economic establishment on notice (DePillis, 2018). Their victories reflect the renewed promise of present-day democracy founded in the evolution from mere hope to genuine revolution.

Perhaps the most obvious examples of this social democratic resurgence have been Jeremy Corbyn in the UK and Bernie Sanders in the US, respectively. They represent an insurgency from within – an opportunity to renew an increasingly ossified democracy. Their proposed renewal is two-fold. The first is the updating of established actually existing democratic practices and norms with a radical anti-establishment energy (Chadwick, 2017). Secondly, they aim to systematically challenge prevailing hegemonic values. They are seeking to directly contradict the belief that there is no alternative to neo-liberalism. Instead they propose that capitalism is both reformable and even potentially replaceable. Quoting Sanders at length, in this regard:

> When I talk about a political revolution, what I am referring to is the need to do more than just win the next election. It's about creating a situation where we are involving millions of people in the process who are not now involved, and changing the nature of media so they are talking about issues that reflect the needs and the pains that so many of our people are currently feeling. A campaign has got to be much more than just getting votes and getting elected. It has got to be helping to educate people, organize people. If we can do that, we can change the dynamic of politics for years and years to come. If 80 to 90 percent of the people in this country vote, if they know what the issues are (and make demands based on that knowledge), Washington and Congress will look very, very different from the Congress currently dominated by big money and dealing only with the issues that big money wants them to deal with. (Sanders, 2015: 344)

Their efforts have been strongly aided and abetted by the innovative use of technology. Returning to the previous examples of Sanders and Corbyn, social media played a huge role in spreading their broader movement and ideology. Here bottom-up democratic empowerment is inexorably linked to harnessing mostly young digitally savvy supporters. Far from being 'armchair activists' as some more traditional prognisticators claim, they have translated their social media passion into concrete campaigning (see Chakelian, 2017). According to noted scholar of youth and politics Sarah Pickard:

> Jeremy Corbyn's leadership election campaign in 2015 (and his re-election in 2016) involved three intertwined factors: mass mobilisations, grassroots support, and digital technologies ... Part of the attraction of Momentum for young people resides in its horizontal, social movement network way of doing politics, as opposed to the rigid, hierarchical Labour Party structure. Similarly, for Momentum sympathisers, the network generates a feeling of belonging to a constructive and positive community that offers hope and potential for change. The very active and interactive use of digital technologies – that comes naturally to many young people – is another part of the appeal and an effective method for both diffusing information and mobilising support. (Pickard, 2017: n.p.)

Similarly, those inspired by the Sanders campaign have begun their own social media-fuelled progressive politics called 'Our Revolution' that embodies the same spirit and aims.

This also extended to more grassroots movements, particularly invigorated efforts to revive industrial democracy linked to wildcat strikes. The so-called 'red state rebellion' which saw teachers across the US heartland in states like West Virginia all the way to Arizona walk out and wage wildcat strikes to demand higher pay epitomises this growing digital democratic insurrection. Hence,

> This is a #MeToo movement, bread and roses, even though it doesn't announce itself as such. Participants, many of whom self-identify as conservative and are Republicans, might even disavow that description. Still, in countless signs, slogans, and messages on social media, teachers in these red states announce that they will be heard. By demanding recognition and respect for their labor and the rights of their students, teachers are reviving the most essential element of labor unionism: respect for democracy and the dignity of work. (Weiner, 2018: n.p.)

Yet this underlying spirit of techno-democratic renewal also has at points a quite conservative character. It harkens back to a social democratic history that combines a desire for the welfare state and a strong union movement. Hence, techno-democracy is often rather Janus faced – looking simultaneously toward an uncertain future and backward to an idealised past.

Techno-Democratic Elitism?

Techno-democratic movements, even amidst their ideological differences, share a commitment to a sense of anti-elitism, at least in principle. In common with techno-populism is a desire to explicitly take on and replace a corrupted and entrenched political and economic ruling class. Yet techno-democracy has a much more complicated relationship with expertise, for admittedly both good and bad. It still invests in the ability of experts to assume and influence democratic leadership and guide progress. It thus rejects present elites while potentially reinforcing the belief in more democratic forms of technocracy.

Significantly, techno-democracy has its roots in actual revolutionary movements. Notably, it took its inspiration from the civil rights movement and more recently the Arab Spring (Khondker, 2011). Ostensibly, this reflected a large-scale rejection of elites (Nineham, 2017). However, it was a revolution waged in part by those who felt educated but underemployed and valued. These same qualities were found in the square protests to a certain extent. Here, educated activists and youth were fighting for social, economic and environmental justice as well as decrying the lack of intelligence of their uninformed democratically elected leaders. This was perhaps the first hi-tech 'smart' revolution, whose 'definining image' is

> a young woman or a young man with a smartphone. She's in the Medina in Tunis with a BlackBerry held aloft, taking a picture of a demonstration outside the prime minister's house. He is an angry Egyptian doctor in an aid station stooping to capture the image of a man with a head injury from missiles thrown by Mubarak's supporters. Or it is a Libyan in Benghazi running with his phone switched to a jerky video mode, surprised when the youth in front of him is shot through the head. All of them are images that have found their way on to the internet through social media sites. And it's not just images. In Tahrir Square I sat one morning next to a 60-year-old surgeon cheerfully tweeting his involvement in the protest. The barricades today do not bristle with bayonets and rifles, but with phones. (Beaumont, 2011)

Nevertheless, techno-democracy also seeks to reorient values of control and accountability. It supports the reversal of traditional control mechanisms.

It is premised on using technology to track the actions and relationship of elites (see for example the activity of the website www.opensecrets.org/ tracking campaign donations of US politicians). For techno-democracy, values of transparency are both prioritised and radicalised. Yet it also must grapple with the question, which it seems to do not enough, with a certain tension at the heart of any and all efforts to achieve greater transparency. This relative paradox of transparency extends to emerging techno-democratic movements as well.

In tracking the economic interests of specific elites, for instance, there can be a distraction from larger ideological questions of the need for elites or top-down forms of leadership itself. There is a risk of fantasising the just and 'ethically clean' leader – one who embodies an almost republican ideal of the wise and disinterred popular rule. This translates to the desire for an uncorrupted techno-democratic leader who is untainted by special interests and uses technology to widen their base of support. It requires politicians charismatic enough and ideologically pure enough to reject elite patronage for popular support.

On the other hand, it aims to establish more democratic cultures. It establishes a growing demand for – often confidential and at times illegally obtained – information about political and economic elites. The most famous of these arguably have been the Panama Papers released by the controversial WikiLeaks and the whistleblower Edward Snowden concerning the widespread but heretofore hidden scale of mass government surveillance in the US. These actions certainly provide the beginnings of a more 'open-sourced' form of democratic politics. They reveal the secrets of power holders, exploiting the technical skill of those would like to expose their misdoings for a mass audience. They present, to this effect, a rebooting of the lauded 'fourth estate', providing a technological update to the traditional watchdog function of what has increasingly become an ideologically compromised and sycophantic mainstream media.

However, as important as these attempts are, they also risk establishing a new democratic technocracy, a collection of tech-savvy organisations and actors who decide what should or should not be publicly released, and what are the ethical norms and limits for such actions. Who decides ultimately the limits of such uncoverings? Who holds these techno-whistleblowers accountable?

Finally, it lends itself to the recapturing of this techno-democratic ethos for the reinforcing of past and future forms of elitism. This is readily apparent in the 'Trumpwashing' mentioned in the previous chapter. They can also be used to support a neoliberal status quo, even while ostensibly protesting the current order. Equally troubling is the justification for these political elites linked to discourses of 'smart' policy – with little to no evidence to sustain such claims.

This is balanced, of course, to an extent by the legitimate faith of techno-democrats in a range of experts, such as scientists informing the climate change debate for example (Kitcher, 2010). Importantly, techno-democrats commonly position themselves as the defenders of these elites against the 'irrational' populist masses.

Tellingly, techno-democracy has also led to novel instances of popular based and even explicitly populist forms of elitism. The electoral success of the Five Star Movement in Italy was derided by the mainstream as another victory for the populist far right. However, often missed in these otherwise legitimate fears, is the strong techno-democratic component of this movement (Deseriis, 2017).

What emerges, then, from these insights is the ironic and complex role that techno-democracy can play in fostering and challenging elites and technocracies. It represents a potent force for technologically expanding democracy as both a concept and practice in the new millennium.

Expanding Techno-Democracy

Technology is not just prospectively renewing and improving democracy but also dramatically expanding its present and future possibilities. In particular it enlarges the demos – who literally and figuratively counts as a democratic citizen while helping to create a 'smarter' demos and widen the potentialities for democratic action. Hence, it is simultaneously reviving democratic norms and pointing to the possibility of completely reinventing them.

At perhaps the most basic level techno-democracy is producing a much larger deliberative civic space. It uses social media and mobile technologies to reintroduce historically marginalised populations as central democratic actors. The Black Lives Matter movement has mobilised resistance against police brutality and systematic racism precisely on this base

(Carney, 2016). In this respect, it serves as a direct counterpoint to the Foucauldian idea of 'biopolitics' – by the governance of the health of the body politic both collectively and personally stating simply, repeatedly, and loudly that their lives and bodies matter, they reveal how restrictive and fraught current democracy is for much of the population it claims to include and represent.

Additionally, it expands the scope and radical potential of e-democracy. It now goes far beyond improving access to service or greater consultation. It now encompasses the reconfiguration of democratic cultures to use community data to transform governance itself (Meijer, 2018), as for example well illustrates the case of Barcelona smart city (Forster, 2018). It creates, in turn, new democratic demands for stronger digital participation and decision-making power. Officially sanctioned programmes such as 'm-voting' in South Korea exemplify this new techno-democratic spirit – allowing people to use their app to informally vote and provide feedback on a range of government proposals.

Gradually being revealed is a potential new dawn for democracy, whether technology refreshes and reinvents power relations, governance and civic society.

The Opportunities of Techno-Democracy

Techno-democracy holds the possibility to change the very ways we theorise, understand and practise democracy. It harkens back to a democratic past while gesturing to an alternative and exciting democratic future. Yet it also can contribute to limiting these democratic possibilities to historic horizons of social democracy while also paradoxically reinforcing the power of present day economic and political elites. Can and how can this tech-driven democracy be truly politically disruptive as opposed to merely socially innovative?

The opportunities of techno-democracy are tantalising and obvious. Notably, it directly connected democratic renewal to pressing demands for economic and social justice. It recaptures, in this regard, the existential power of democracy – its ability to grant people the agency to choose their form of existence rather than be told there is no alternative. This is fuelled by ICTs that permit a more inclusive, networked and participatory democratic culture.

However, it also poses profound challenges. These moments struggle with the understandable embrace of a range of knowledge expertise with the threat of configuring and creating new democratic technocracies. Ideologically, it remains trapped to a worrying degree in the ideas of the 20th century, aiming to revive the welfare state and industrial democracy. It is in this respect as much about recapturing democracy as it is reinventing it.

At stake though are clear distinguishing features of techno-democracy as a force to oppose techno-populism. Techno-democracy is about greater inclusion and the expansion of democratic power, rather than simply the representing of the 'people' and the replacement of one set of elites for another. It concerns the expansion of human and democratic rights. Critical, however, is again whether they are simply reviving traditional solutions to new problems or coming up with new ones. Importantly, the question of whether this is disruptive or innovative is not to assume that to be innovative is in and of itself all bad. It certainly challenges how limited the current democratic imaginary remains – showing the need to extend basic democratic rights to still disenfranchised groups and reintroducing democracy as a 'revolutionary' social force. Again, after decades of being told that we had reached the end of history, suddenly everyone is looking to the future for something radically different.

5

LOOKING FORWARD TO
DISRUPTIVE DEMOCRACY

The new millenium could spell the end of democracy or its radical renewal. Any optimism for its future is inexorably intertwined with its ability to become once more a force for revolutionising social, economic and political relations. At present, it remains trapped between the two poles of either supporting or partially interrupting a broken status quo. It doubles as an elite resource or a tool for resistance. What it is only now beginning to recapture is its fundamentally existential spirit and power, its role as a historical vehicle for people to critically and collectively transform their very shared existence. To do so, it must become a disruptive political technology.

The need for such a disruptive democracy has arguably never been so urgent. The threat of an exploitive industry 4.0 looms large. It is telling that advances in AI, big data, the Internet of Things, and virtual reality conjure up as much fear as they do excitement. Just as at the outset of the first industrial revolution, we are once again arriving at a crossroads of history. It will almost certainly be completely technologically rebooted. In the 19th century this demanded the creation and evolution of novel political democratic technologies to counter, cope with and transform this growing and all-encompassing capitalist reality. The pressing question is, can 21st century democracy be updated and refreshed to similarly respond to and meet these new capitalist challenges?

Absolutely crucial, is that this does not become confined to mere social innovations. Undeniably, the protection of basic democratic rights and norms is vital. For democracy to survive and society to progress, it must do more than simply seek to defend and recapture past gains. It must move beyond merely extending its traditional franchise to all people in both principle and fact. Instead it must democratise how we use and benefit from technology, in the process expanding our individual and collective human potential.

Democracy 4.0?

We are supposedly at the cusp of a new and total economic revolution. It will bring to the fore rapidly advancing technologies in a way that could inalterably reshape social relations and shatter our traditional social contract. Indeed the

> [p]revious industrial revolutions liberated humankind from animal power, made mass production possible and brought digital capabilities to billions of people. This Fourth Industrial Revolution is, however, fundamentally different. It is characterized by a range of new technologies that are fusing the physical, digital and biological worlds, impacting all disciplines, economies and industries, and even challenging ideas about what it means to be human. (Schwab, 2016)

Yet it is also a distinct opportunity for producing democracy 4.0.

While it is common to think of economic development and associated stages of capitalism, this same sense of dynamic growth and evolution is rarely applied to democracy. Perhaps the closest comparisons are notions of different chronological democratic waves (see Diamond, 1996). However, this chronological and geographical based perspective risks missing the deeper changes to democracy both in terms of its overall purpose and specific processes within the modern era. They are briefly:

- the revolutionary stage following the liberal revolutions and the industrial revolution;
- the social democratic stage starting roughly at the turn of the 20th century in which social and economic rights became democratically enshrined;
- the liberal stage in which human and social rights were expanded alongside the spread of the free market.

Each of these stages reflected a particular historical instance of democratisation. The first was the need to expand the right for authority and power to be subject to popular consent. The second was the effort to place the social and economic spheres under similar democratic control. The third and most recent stage was the demand that democratic and human rights be made universal and as such create a more inclusive and representative governance both politically and economically.

Each of these instances of democratisation, moreover, was born out of the one that came before it. The managing ethos of the initial stage was directly premised on the need to establish popular control in the wake of a half century of previous social upheavals and revolution. This political need played into and drew inspiration from the early capitalist attempts to discipline a newly industrialising workforce both at home and in the colonies (see for instance Mintz, 1986). Yet it was precisely this management spirit and reality that led to a new stage of democracy – one that asked why it was not also possible to manage social resources for the public good? This catalysed the progressive and political labour movements into the creation of social democracies and the welfare state. However, the legacies of racism, sexism and classism persisted, thus opening up this new socialised form of democracy to legitimate and profound criticisms. The most current stage, hence, focuses on the requirement to make democracy both inclusive and universal.

Revealed in this admittedly very brief history as well is the complex and intimate relationship between democracy in the formal political sphere and within the broader cultural and economic ones. The labour struggles of the late 19th century against economic management helped build the political movements and coalitions for social democracy mere decades later. It provided workers with the knowledge and tools necessary for organising themselves as a group and engaging in difficult political negotiations of democratic power-sharing. Conversely, the call for greater inclusiveness, representation and diversity offered latter day capitalists the discourses and tools to refashion themselves as 'progressive' actors seeking to create more multicultural, meritocratic and people-centred institutions and economies. Further, it shifted the debate from enlarging social equality to expanding financial inclusion.

At stake, then, is how democracy is always a historically specific phenomenon that is usually at once both socially innovative and politically disruptive. For it to advance forward it should build on the structural economic and social contradictions of its present moment and effectively identify and politicise its arising forms of struggle for the creation of something culturally new. In the contemporary era this entails recognising calls for people to have equal access to the material and social capital to shape their own personal economic destiny in a way that allows them to radically exploit new technologies for this purpose. Hence, democracy 4.0 will be premised upon the core disruptive values of radical openness, personalisation and emancipation.

Democratising the Future

The task of present day democracy must be to an extent completely reoriented. It is not how it can be saved or even renewed. Instead, it is what role it can play in democratising the future. More precisely, how can it turn contemporary grievances into a forward thinking politics that both inspires political hope, expands our concrete possibilities and reduces the forces of social domination?

Critical, in this respect, is expanding upon and ultimately transcending a politics of inclusion. It requires respecting but ultimately going beyond demands of inclusiveness for a society of openness. The ethos of openness asks for more than just including subjects in an existing social order – whether democratic, liberal, or otherwise. The previous chapter discussed the potential creation of more 'open source' democracies centred on the mass release of information about the actions and misdoings of elites. At present this remains largely a whistleblowing activity and about those that can fit relatively comfortably in principle (though certainly not in practice as recent history starkly reveals) within existing liberal notions of transparency (Fung et al., 2007). In a recent interview, Edward Snowden's lawyer, Robert Tibbo, declared:

> ... working with Mr Snowden you come in contact with – in a very significant way – with fundamental rights and freedoms, such as freedom of expression, association, assembly, and this all comes back to how our lives, our private lives are affected, our personal lives, such as freedom of thought, conscience, and freedom of religion, mobility. How we practice our religion comes out of freedom of expression. What clothes we wear, where we pray, where we congregate, where we assemble. Working with Mr Snowden, you realise how significant his disclosures are, and the impact of government enacting greater security laws and how it effects people, and how people have modified their behaviour ... Fear, people have a fear in expressing themselves. It [mass surveillance] has had what I call a constructive violation of people's fundamental rights, such as

expression, assembly, association and religion. Snowden's revelations are the most significant for this century so far. (quoted in Munro, 2017: 109)

However, it is also expanding in quite radical directions. Blockchains and time stamping, for instance, can track the labour practices of major corporations in real time. In a recent 2017 report to the European Parliament these implications were made clear, as it was noted that Blockchain

> makes it possible to establish and maintain complete ownership histories, which can help counteract fraud and support police and insurance investigators tracking stolen gems. It also allows consumers to make more informed purchasing decisions, e.g. to limit their search to diamonds with a clean history that is free from fraud, theft, forced labour and the intervention of dubious vendors who are linked to violence, drugs or arms trafficking. (Boucher, 2017: 16).

Similarly, these same technologies can be potentially deployed to expose how big banks and financial institutions are being capitally funded and how major economic actors avoid and evade taxes. Even *Forbes* magazine noted its potential, in this respect, in relation to the IRS (Internal Revenue Service), the tax collection agency of the United States federal government:

> Blockchain and its digital ledger platform can revolutionize the way data is analyzed, exchanged and stored by the IRS. Blockchain can help the IRS lower costs and increase security, as well as enhance the speed in which it accesses and reviews taxpayer data. Here are just a few small examples of some of the issues the IRS is currently experiencing. (Bergman, 2018: n.p.)

There are also more politically disruptive implications offered by this emphasis on openness rather than simple inclusion. It is the capacity to reimagine and select between different alternative futures. Here, inclusion is an engine for allowing marginalised groups to have their voices heard in shaping the present and future. It also means opening up these potentialities – turning what is considered into the plausible. In her viral campaign video, recently elected Congressperson democratic socialist Alexandria Ocasio-Cortez passionately pushed back against the seemingly 'idealistic demands' being put forward by progressives. She proclaims that what is needed is 'Medicaid for all, tuition free college, a federal jobs guarantee, and criminal justice reform. We can do it now. It does not take a hundred years to do this. It takes political courage.'

While these policies are not in and of themselves revolutionary, they starkly reveal an emerging democratic spirit that rails against neoliberal politicians who claim even such basic social democratic reforms are economically and politically impossible. This sets the stage for more robust contemporary debates and movements for ensuring that tomorrow's world is decided democratically rather than being framed as an unavoidable economic inevitability.

These disruptive possibilities also encompass the need to go beyond identity politics. Importantly, this is not meant to repeat or reinforce the now familiar leftist critique of identity based politics for one that focuses on class struggle and economic justice. Conversely, it stresses the expansion of the possibility of identity as a form of social liberation and radical exploration. Theories of intersectionality touch on the expansive and disruptive potentialities of such a revolutionary form of identity politics. It speaks of multiple selves, focusing on the diverse ways people face discrimination. The contemporary era is witnessing

> the reformulation of the self as a site constituted and fragmented, at least partially, by the intersections of various categories of domination/oppression such as race, gender, and sexual orientation. Thus, far from being a unitary and static phenomenon untainted by experience, one's core identity is made up of the various discourses and structures that shape society and one's experience within it. (Powell, 1996: 1484)

Digital technologies allow people to use this as a basis to explore multiple forms of self-hoods (Bloom, 2019). In this regard, technology can become a force for allowing people to engage with and experience multiple identities over the course of their lifetime. This speaks to Donna Haraway's revolutionary 'Cyborg Manifesto', in which she declares

> Cyborg writing must not be about the Fall, the imagination of a once-upon-a-time wholeness before language, before writing, before Man. Cyborg writing is about the power to survive, not on the basis of original innocence, but on the basis of seizing the tools to mark the world that marked them as other. (Haraway, [1985] 2016: 55)

Going even further, in this regard, is the ability of all individuals, especially those in historically excluded groups, to repurpose and reuse technologies to take back control of their identity and experiment with alternative modes of social relations. The recent landmark book by Helen Hester, *Xenofeminism*, proposes 'a technomaterialist, anti-naturalist, and gender abolitionist form of feminism' (2018: 1). She argues thus:

> any emancipatory techno-feminism must take the form of a concerted political intervention, sensitive to the fused character of the structures of oppression that make up our material world. It is in this spirit that xenofeminism seeks to balance an attentiveness to the differential impact that technology can have on gender, queers, and gender non-conforming with a critical openness (to the constrained but genuine) transformative potential of technologies. (Hester, 2018: 11)

This politics of openness and abolitionism demands, in turn, a democratic ethos that avowedly goes beyond reformism. It entails constructing movements and political processes that are charged with developing systematic change in both their vision, policy proposals and actions. The appeal to social democracy should serve as a springboard for more emancipatory social and economic alternatives. It means expanding our critical imagination to reconceive economy and society. To this end, acclaimed theorist Will Davies writes of the possibility of 'economic science fictions', asking

> Is it still possible to go back in search of the future? ... To write science fictions about the economy is to insist on the possibility that imagination can intrude into economic life in an uninvited way that is not computable or accountable. To imagine wholly different systems and premises of calculation, for example, is in itself to resist the dystopian ideal promised by Wall Street and Silicon Valley, that there is nothing that can evade the logic of software algorithms, risk, and finance. At a time when capitalism and socialism have collapsed into each other, obliterating spaces of alterity or uncalculated discourses in the process, simply to describe unrealised (maybe unrealistic) economic possibilities is to rediscover a glimpse of autonomy in the process. (Davies, 2018: 22)

Crucial for all these future-oriented politics is the radical democratisation of the present. ICTs have produced novel modes of power. Arising is what can be termed 'virtual power'. Hence, while these distinct but connected political disruptions do not always explicitly speak to the expansion of democracy, they share a commitment to a dramatic democratisation of contemporary and prospective socio-economic relations, linked to the disruptive potential of democracy.

Disrupting Democratic Power

Current technologies contain the seeds of new radical presents and futures to bloom and flourish. Advances in ICTs connect people with power in such a way as to reveal their capability for not only improving but also completely transforming their social existence. Yet these incipient ideas and revolutionary struggles do not necessarily explicitly speak to how they could be democratically realised or in what way existing democratic norms and practices will need to be updated to meet these revolutionary opportunities and challenges.

Fortunately, there are vibrant democratic movements and technologies that are pointing toward a future that is simultaneously radical and democratic. Civic technologies – commonly referred to as Civtech – open the space for empowering and reconceiving public participation for 21st century democracy and the reach of democratic power (e.g. Fung, 2004; Nabatchi and Leighninger, 2015; Tsagarousianou et al., 2002.) They explicitly use ICT and big data for addressing 'global' public affairs challenges (Mergel et al., 2016). These technologies are reinforced by the development of social technologies that encourage the fostering of 'participatory futures' (Meijer, 2012). This technologically rebooted civic culture can help to inform existing experimentation with radical democratic community building around the world. It opens up the possibility for digital networking and political activism in a glocalised public sphere where leaders and politicised civil society organisations (Della Porta, 2018) may engage in a new progressive world politics inspired by global human advancement and by a new humanism. It also offers the possibility of creating more exportable models for drawing upon these technologies to promote radically democratic forms of politics and life. Such a radical experiment is being launched in Taiwan by its self-proclaimed 'hacker minister' Audrey Tang. She helped launch 'vTaiwan'

> experimenting with bringing citizens and public servants together in a civic deliberation process utilising state of the art technologies for crafting digital legislation. The adoption of these technologies brings a more transparent, responsive, and participatory deliberation process, which is the core of public participation and the open government movement. By openly aggregating shared wisdom from the society on a regular basis, the experiments created a recursive public, an open and interactive community environment that kept track of [an] updated rough consensus for crafting legislation and regulation. (Lin, 2018: n.p.)

There is further need to transform the democratisation of technology into novel types of democratic rights and responsibilities linked to technological exploration. The recent work on trans-humanism and the enhancement of human capabilities speaks directly to these themes. In his celebrated book *SuperIntelligence*, philosopher Nick Bostrom concludes the following:

(1) at least weak forms of superintelligence are achievable by means of biotech-nological enhancements; (2) the feasibility of cognitively enhanced humans adds to the plausibility that advanced forms of machine intelligence are feasible—because even if we were fundamentally unable to create machine intelligence (which there is no reason to suppose), machine intelligence might still be within reach of cognitively enhanced humans; and (3) when we con-sider scenarios stretching significantly into the second half of this century and beyond, we must take into account the probable emergence of a generation of genetically enhanced populations—voters, inventors, scientists—with the mag-nitude of enhancement escalating rapidly over subsequent decades. (Bostrom, 2014: 44)

These themes additionally bring to the fore serious philosophical concerns of how to balance the radical potentialities of technologies with broader questions of social responsibility and non-harm. It is precisely to this debate that James Hughes' (2004) influential book *Citizen Cyborg* remains so timely and relevant a contribution. He maps out an updated vision of citizenship that, as suggested by the title, revolves around the use of tech-nology for expanding human potentiality.

Finally, the radical re-envisioning of the future gestures toward the possibilities of fostering a more explicitly democratic form of what can be termed virtual governance. Technology is progressively allowing people to immersively experience a wide range of alternative realities. Building on these efforts are more directly political or at least socially empowering pro-jects in which mobile technology is used to expand local knowledge as well as foster solidarity within and among marginalised groups across the globe in a glocal perspective, where a global civil society is networked to foster a collective (Ospina and Foldy, 2015) and place-based leadership (Jackson and Parry, 2011) action towards democratic and public value aims (Crosby and Bryson, 2005).

The revolutionary implications of these virtual advancements are equally profound and democratic. One can now just begin to imagine a politics in which realtime data is mixed with hi-tech virtual simulations to allow people to 'experience' different social options and make democratic choices on this basis. Think for instance if referendums such as Brexit were informed not just by competing ideologies or projections of what might happen but also by immersive experiences that would realistically allow people to explore these different futures from a range of diverse first person perspectives.

Even more radically, perhaps, is the virtual creation of alternative societies linked to 'post-capitalism' or a 'world without prisons' permitting individuals and groups to 'experience' what a more radical future may look and feel like. This opportunity to virtually time travel could transform the revolution from an exercise in resistance and vague premonitions of a better tomorrow to come, into vibrant virtual scenarios that actively challenge the limits of our present day concrete existence. (Bloom, 2016b). These technological interventions would serve as the foundations for reimagining and democratically struggling for more liberated and emancipated worlds.

The Real Possibilities of Disruptive Democracy

This book highlights the coming clash between techno-populism and techno-democracy. Neoliberalism and the free market continue to face a deep ideological, political and existential crisis. Arising in its place are 'techno-politics' that stress the rights of re-empowered people and citizens to take power and control their collective social destinies. Each shares a rejection of the establishment and a desire to exploit and repurpose technology for this politically disruptive purpose. Yet while techno-populism is clinging to essentialised identities and increasingly hi-tech autocratic rule, techno-democracy holds the promise of reinventing social, economic and political relations in a more open and egalitarian way. Nevertheless, this revolutionary potential is put at risk through a continual embrace of 20th century political solutions and knowledge in a brave new 21st century world.

These insights serve to technologically revolutionise existing theories of radical democracy. Laclau and Mouffe end their famous book on hegemony with a novel perspective for radicalising democratic relations. Mouffe, in particular, has developed these ideas into a model democracy that stresses values of agonism, the allowance for radical difference within a shared democratic framework of norms and values. What this work proposes, building on but ultimately seeking to transcend these ideas, is the need to understand democracy as composed of a set of social technologies that have the potential to reinforce or disrupt hegemony. The question here is how can these technologies be used to democratise and politically expand the limits of social possibility? Can they create radically new fields of meaning that retain a commitment to core democratic values of openness, equality and collective power?

For techno-democracy to survive and thrive it must do more than be satisfied with remaining simply a socially innovative technology. Instead it is imperative for it to strengthen its commitment to its radical potential. Democracy should stand for new ways of organising, decision-making, and recreating our economic material relations and social realities. At its most revolutionary, democracy can still transform the very ways we govern ourselves (Fung, 2016) and experiment with ways of existing in the world. In the midst of so much political uncertainty, social anxiety and economic insecurity – faced with an industrial revolution that augurs our literal and figurative dehumanisation – can democracy once more become a disruptive force for revolutionary optimism?

REFERENCES

Akpan, N. (2016) Here's how hackers might mess with electronic voting on Election Day. PBS News Hour, 8 November. Retrieved from www.pbs.org/newshour/science/heres-how-hackers-could-mess-with-electronic-voting.

Andersen, T., Jensen, P. and Skovsgaard, C. (2016) The heavy plow and the agricultural revolution in Medieval Europe. *Journal of Development Economics*, *118*: 133–49. doi: 10.1016/j.jdeveco.2015.08.006.

Andrejevic, M. and Gates, K. (2014) Big data surveillance: Introduction. *Surveillance & Society*, *12* (2): 185–96. doi: 10.24908/ss.v12i2.5242.

Andrews, L. (2018) Public administration, public leadership and the construction of public value in the age of the algorithm and 'big data'. *Public Administration*. E-pub ahead of print doi: 10.1111/padm.12534.

Ansell, C. and Trondal, J. (2017) Governing turbulence: An organizational-institutional agenda. *Perspectives on Public Management and Governance, 1* (1): 43–57. doi: 10.1093/ppmgov/gvx013.

Badiou, A. and Feltham, O. (1987) *Being and Event*. London: Continuum.

Barber, B. (1992) Jihad vs. McWorld. *The Atlantic Monthly*, 269(3): 53–65.

BBC News (2018) Elon Musk unveils first tourist for SpaceX 'Moon loop'. BBC News Science & Environment, 18 September. Retrieved from www.bbc.co.uk/news/science-environment-45550755.

Beal, G. M., and Bohlen, J. M. (1957) *The Diffusion Process*. Agricultural Experiment Station, Iowa State College.

Beaumont, P. (2011) 'The Truth about Twitter, Facebook and the Uprisings in the Arab World', *The Guardian*, 25 February.

Beckett, F. (2010) *What Did the Baby Boomers Ever Do for Us?* London: Biteback.

Bergman, A. (2018) How blockchain technology can save the IRS. *Forbes*, 4 June. Retrieved from www.forbes.com/sites/greatspeculations/2018/06/04/how-blockchain-technology-can-save-the-irs/#5a12f026e7ab.

Bertoni, S. (2017) Jared Kushner in his own words on the Trump data operation the FBI is reportedly probing. *Forbes*, 26 May. Retrieved from www.forbes.com/sites/stevenbertoni/2017/05/26/jared-kushner-in-his-own-words-on-the-trump-data-operation-the-fbi-is-reportedly-probing/#6186ae5da90f.

Beynon, H. (2014) 'Still too much socialism in Britain': The legacy of Margaret Thatcher. *Industrial Relations Journal, 45* (3): 214–33. doi: 10.1111/irj.12051.

Bloom, P. (2016a) *Authoritarian Capitalism in the Age of Globalization*. Cheltenham: Edward Elgar.

Bloom, P. (2016b) *Beyond Power and Resistance: Politics at the Radical Limits*. New York: Rowman and Littlefield International

Bloom, P. (2018) *The Bad Faith in the Free Market: The Radical Promise of Existential Freedom*. Cham: Palgrave Macmillan/Springer Nature.

Bloom, P. (2019) *Monitored: Business and Surveillance in the Time of Big Data*. London: Pluto Press.

Bloom, P. and Dallyn, S. (2011) The paradox of order: reimagining ideological domination. *Journal of Political Ideologies*, *16*(01): 53–78.

Bloom, P. and Rhodes, C. (2017) Political Leadership in the 21st Century: NeoLiberalism and the Rise of the CEO Politician. *The Routledge Companion to Leadership*. Abingdon: Routledge.

Bloom, P. and Rhodes, C. (2018) *CEO Society: The Corporate Takeover of Everyday Life*. London: Zed.

Blumler, J. G. (2003) Foreword: Broadening and Deepening Comparative Research. In G. Mazzoleni, J. Stewart and B. Horsfield (eds), *The Media and Neo-populism: A contemporary comparative analysis*. Westport, CT: Praeger.

Bock, P. (2017) The startup president: how Macron built a party like a business—and conquered France, *Prospect*. Retrieved from https://www.prospectmagazine.co.uk/politics/the-startup-president-how-macron-built-a-party-like-a-business-and-conquered-france.

Bonefeld, W., Gunn, R. and Psychopedis, K. (1992) *Open Marxism Volume 1: Dialectics and History*. London: Pluto Press.

Bostrom, N. (2014) *Superintelligence: Paths, Dangers, Strategies*. Oxford: Oxford University Press.

Botsman, R. (2017) Big data meets Big Brother as China moves to rate its citizens, *WIRED*, 21 October. Retrieved from www.wired.co.uk/article/chinese-government-social-credit-score-privacy-invasion.

Boucher, P. (2017) How blockchain technology could change our lives. Retrieved from www.europarl.europa.eu/RegData/etudes/IDAN/2017/581948/EPRS_IDA(2017)581948_EN.pdf.

Brandsen, T., Trommel, W. and Verschuere, B. (eds) (2014) *Manufactured Civil Society: Practices, Principles and Effects*. London: Palgrave.

Braverman, H. (1974) *Labor and Monopoly Capitalism*. New York: Monthly Review.

Brown, W. (2016) *Undoing the Demos*. New York: Zone Books.

Bryson, J., Sancino, A., Benington, J. and Sørensen, E. (2016) Towards a multi-actor theory of public value co-creation. *Public Management Review*, *19* (5): 640–54. doi: 10.1080/14719037.2016.1192164.

Cadwalladr, C. (2017) The Great British Brexit Robbery: How our democracy was hijacked, *The Guardian*, 7 May. Retrieved from www.theguardian.com/technology/2017/may/07/the-great-british-brexit-robbery-hijacked-democracy.

Caiani, M. and Graziano, P. (2016) Varieties of populism: insights from the Italian case. *Italian Political Science Review/Rivista Italiana Di Scienza Politica*, *46* (2): 243–67. doi: 10.1017/ipo.2016.6.

Canovan, M. (1982) Two strategies for the study of populism. *Political Studies*, *30* (4): 544–52. doi: 10.1111/j.1467-9248.1982.tb00559.x.

Carney, N. (2016) All lives matter, but so does race. *Humanity & Society*, *40* (2): 180–99. doi: 10.1177/0160597616643868.

Castells, M. (1997) *The Rise of the Network Society*. Malden, MA: Wiley–Blackwell.

Cederström, C. and Spicer, A. (2017) *The Wellness Syndrome*. Cambridge: Polity Press.

Chadwick, A. (2017) Corbyn, Labour, digital media, and the 2017 UK election. In E. Thorsen, D. Jackson and D. Lilleker (eds), *UK Election Analysis 2017: Media, Voters and the Campaign: Early Reflections from Leading Academics*. Poole: The Centre for the Study of Journalism, Culture and Community, Bournemouth University. p. 89.

Chaeklin, A. (2017) 'The Manifesto Won it' *Progress Magazine* 12 July.

Chomsky, N. (1998) *The Common Good*. Tucson, AZ: Odonian Press.

CNN (1998) Explosive Starr report outlines case for impeachment. Investigating the President, 11 September. Retrieved from http://edition.cnn.com/ALLPOLITICS/stories/1998/09/11/starr.report/.

Cooke, B. and Kothari, U. (2001) *Participation: The New Tyranny?* London: Zed.

Costanza-Chock, S. (2012) Mic check! Media cultures and the Occupy Movement. *Social Movement Studies*, *11* (3–4): 375–85. doi: 10.1080/14742837.2012.710746.

Crosby, B.C. and Bryson, J.M. (2005) *Leadership for the Common Good*. Chichester: Wiley.

Davies, W. (ed.) (2018) *Economic Science Fictions*. London: Goldsmiths Press.

Della Porta, D. (2018) Innovations from below: Civil society beyond the crisis. In *International Society for Third Sector Research Conference*, Free University of Amsterdam.

Demmers, J., Fernandez Jilberto, A. and Hogenboom, B. (2004) *Good Governance in the Era of Global Neoliberalism*. London: Routledge.

DePillis, L. (2018) White House issues 70-page rebuttal to rise of socialist economics. Retrieved from https://edition.cnn.com/2018/10/23/economy/cea-socialism/index.html.

Deseriis, M. (2017) Direct parliamentarianism: An analysis of the political values embedded in Rousseau, the 'Operating System' of the Five Star Movement. *Jedem – Ejournal of Edemocracy and Open Government*, *9* (2): 47–67. doi: 10.29379/jedem.v9i2.471.

Deudney, D. and Ikenberry, G. J. (2009) The myth of the autocratic revival: Why liberal democracy will prevail. *Foreign Affairs*, *88*(1): 77–93.

Dey, P. and Teasdale, S. (2015) Deviance, ignorance and the 'Art of Governing': Revisiting post-Foucauldian governmentality studies. In *7th International Social Innovation Research Conference (ISIRC)*, York, UK.

Diamond, L. (1996) Is the Third Wave over? *Journal of Democracy*, *7* (3): 20–37. doi: 10.1353/jod.1996.0047.

Etter, L. (2017) What happens when the government uses Facebook as a weapon? *Bloomberg Business Week*, 7 December. Retrieved from www.bloomberg.com/news/features/2017-12-07/how-rodrigo-duterte-turned-facebook-into-a-weapon-with-a-little-help-from-facebook.

Faye, J. (1996) *Le Siecle des Ideologies*. Paris: Arman Colin.

Ferlie, E., Fitzgerald, L. and Pettigrew, A. (1996) *The New Public Management in Action*. Oxford: Oxford University Press.

Fisher, W. (1982) Romantic democracy, Ronald Reagan, and presidential heroes. *Western Journal of Speech Communication*, *46* (3): 299–310. doi: 10.1080/10570318209374088.

Flinders, M. (2015) The problem with democracy. *Parliamentary Affairs*, *69* (1): 181–203. doi: 10.1093/pa/gsv008.

Flinders, M. and Wood, M. (2014) Depoliticisation, governance and the state. *Policy & Politics*, *42* (2): 135–49. doi: 10.1332/030557312x655873.

Flood, A. (2016) 'Post-truth' named word of the year by Oxford Dictionaries. *The Guardian*, 15 November. Retrieved from www.theguardian.com/books/2016/nov/15/post-truth-named-word-of-the-year-by-oxford-dictionaries.

Forket, K. (2014) The new moralism: Austerity, silencing and debt morality. *Soundings*, (*56*): 41–530.

Forster, R. (2018) How Barcelona's smart city strategy is giving 'power to the people'. Retrieved from https://cities-today.com/power-to-the-people/.

Foucault, M. (1991) Governmentality. In G. Burchell, C. Gordon and P. Miller (eds), *The Foucault Effect: Studies in Governmentality*. Chicago: University of Chicago Press. pp. 87–104.

Foucault, M. and Sheridan, A. (1979) *Discipline and Punish*. London: Penguin Books.

Foucault, M., Martin, L., Gutman, H. and Hutton, P. (1982) *Technologies of the Self*. Amherst, MA: University of Massachusetts Press.

Friedman, U. (2017) What is a populist? And is Donald Trump one? *The Atlantic*, 27 February. Retrieved from www.theatlantic.com/international/archive/2017/02/what-is-populist-trump/516525/

Fuchs, C. (2018) *Digital Demagogue*. London: Pluto Press.

Fukuyama, F. (1989) The end of history? *The National Interest*, (16): 3–18.

Fung, A. (2004) *Empowered Participation*. Princeton, NJ: Princeton University Press.

Fung, A. (2016) Our desperate need to save US democracy from ourselves. *The Hill*, 7 December. Retrieved from https://thehill.com/blogs/pundits-blog/presidential-campaign/309232-our-desperate-need-to-save-american-democracy-from.

Fung, A., Graham, M. and Weil, D. (2007) *Full Disclosure: The Perils and Promise of Transparency*. Cambridge: Cambridge University Press.

Ganuza, E. and Baiocchi, G. (2018) The power of ambiguity: How participatory budgeting travels the globe. Retrieved from www.publicdeliberation.net/jpd/vol8/iss2/art8/.

Gendron, G. (2017). Quartiers populaires: Macron, chasseur de têtes. *Libération*, 30 March.

Giddens, A. (1984) *The Constitution of Society*. Cambridge: Polity Press.

Gilbert, J. (2013) What kind of thing is 'neoliberalism'? *New Formations*, *80* (80): 7–22. doi: 10.3898/newf.80/81.introduction.2013.

Glynos, J. and Howarth, D. (2008) *Logics of Critical Explanation in Social and Political Theory*. London: Routledge.

Gramsci, A. and Hoare, Q. (1971) *Selections from the Prison Notebooks of Antonio Gramsci*. London: Lawrence and Wishart.

Grint, K. (2005) *Leadership: Limits and Possibilities*. London/Basingstoke: Palgrave Macmillan.

Harari, Y. (2018) Why technology favors tyranny. *The Atlantic*, October. Retrieved from www.theatlantic.com/magazine/archive/2018/10/yuval-noah-harari-technology-tyranny/568330/.

Haraway, D. ([1985] 2016) A cyborg manifesto: Science, technology and socialist feminism in the late twentieth century. In *Manifestly Haraway*. University of Minnesota Press. Retrieved from https://tinyurl.com/y7lhog6s.

Harvey, D. (2005) *A Brief History of Neoliberalism*. Oxford: Oxford University Press.

Hendrickson, C. and Galston, W. (2017) Why are populists winning online? Social media reinforces their anti-establishment message. Brookings, 28 April. Retrieved from https://www.brookings.edu/blog/techtank/2017/04/28/why-are-populists-winning-online-social-media-reinforces-their-anti-establishment-message/.

Henry, Z. (2017). How Emmanuel Macron aims to make France a "Startup Nation".. *Inc.*, 15 June .

Herszenhorn, D. (2018) Congress approves $700 billion Wall Street bailout. *New York Times*, 3 October. Retrieved from www.nytimes.com/2008/10/03/business/worldbusiness/03iht-bailout.4.16679355.html.

Hester, H. (2018) *Xenofeminism*. Cambridge: Polity Press.

Hickey, S. and Mohan, G. (2005) Relocating participation within a radical politics of development. *Development and Change, 36* (2): 237–62. doi: 10.1111/j.0012-155x.2005.00410.x.

Hild, M. (2007) *Greenbackers, Knights of Labor, and Populists*. Athens, GA: University of Georgia Press.

Hoover, K. (1987) The rise of conservative capitalism: Ideological tensions within the Reagan and Thatcher Governments. *Comparative Studies in Society and History, 29* (2): 245. doi: 10.1017/s0010417500014493.

Howard, M. (2001) E-government across the globe: How will 'e' change government. *E-Government, 90*: 80.

Howarth, D. (2000) *Discourse*. Buckingham: Open University Press.

Hughes, J. (2004) *Citizen Cyborg: Why Democratic Societies Must Respond to the Redesigned Human of the Future*. Boulder, CO: Westview Press.

Huntington, S. (1993) The clash of civilizations? *Foreign Affairs, 72* (3): 22. doi: 10.2307/20045621.

Illing. S. (2018) Why capitalism won't survive without socialism, *Vox*, 4 July. Retrived from https://www.vox.com/policy-and-politics/2017/7/25/15998002/eric-weinstein-capitalism-socialism-revolution.

Jackson, B. and Parry, K. (2011) *A Very Short, Fairly Interesting and Reasonably Cheap Book about Studying Leadership*, 2nd edn. Los Angeles, CA: Sage.

Jenson, J. and Harrison, D. (2013) Social innovation research in the European Union: approaches, findings and future directions. In European Commission (ed.), *Policy Review*. Luxembourg: Publication Office of the European Union.

Kahn, R. and Kellner, D. (2004) New Media and internet activism: From the 'Battle of Seattle' to blogging. *New Media & Society*, *6* (1): 87–95. doi: 10.1177/1461444804039908.

Kattel, R. and Mergel, I. (2018) Is Estonia the Silicon Valley of digital government? UCL IIPP Blog, 28 September. Retrieved from https://medium.com/iipp-blog/is-estonia-the-silicon-valley-of-digital-government-bf15adc8e1ea.

Keane, J. (2011) Monitory democracy. In S. Alonso, J. Keane and W. Merkel (eds), *The Future of Representative Democracy*. Cambridge: Cambridge University Press. pp. 212–35.

Khondker, H. (2011) Role of the New Media in the Arab Spring. *Globalizations*, *8* (5): 675–9. doi: 10.1080/14747731.2011.621287.

King, C., Stivers, C. and Box, R. (1998) *Government Is Us*. London: Sage.

Kirzner, I. M. (1999) Creativity and/or alertness: A reconsideration of the Schumpeterian entrepreneur. *The Review of Austrian Economics*, *11*(1–2): 5–17.

Kitcher, P. (2010) The climate change debate. *Science*, *328*: 1230–4.

Krahnke, K., Giacalone, R. and Jurkiewicz, C. (2003) Point–counterpoint: Measuring workplace spirituality. *Journal of Organizational Change Management*, *16* (4): 396–405. doi: 10.1108/09534810310484154.

Laclau, E. (1996). *Emancipation(s)*. New York: Verso.

Laclau, E. (2007) *On Populist Reason*. New York: Verso.

Laclau, E. and Mouffe, C. (1986) *Hegemony and Socialist Strategy*. London: Verso.

Laclau, E. and Mouffe, C. (1987) Post-Marxism without apologies. *New Left Review*, I166.

Latour, B. (2005) *Reassembling the Social: An Introduction to Actor-Network Theory*. Oxford: Oxford University Press.

Leibetseder, B. (2011) A critical review on the concept of social technology. *Social Technologies*, *1* (1): 7–24.

Lin, S. (2018) How Taiwan's online democracy may show future of humans and machines. *Sydney Morning Herald*, 9 August. Retrieved from www.smh.com.au/technology/how-taiwan-s-online-democracy-may-show-future-of-humans-and-machines-20180809-p4zwe1.html.

Ma, A. (2018) China has started ranking citizens with a creepy 'social credit' system – here's what you can do wrong, and the embarrassing, demeaning ways they can punish you. *Business Insider*, 29 October. Retrieved from http://uk.businessinsider.com/china-social-credit-system-punishments-and-rewards-explained-2018-4.

Macron, E. (2017) *Révolution*. Paris: Pocket

Magatti, M. (2017) *Cambio di paradigma: uscire dalla crisi pensando il futuro*. Milan: Feltrinelli Editore.

Mann, S. and Ferenbok, J. (2013) New Media and the power politics of sousveillance in a surveillance-dominated world. *Surveillance & Society*, *11* (1/2): 18–34. doi: 10.24908/ss.v11i1/2.4456.

Marchart, O. (2007) *Post-Foundational Political Thought*. Edinburgh: Edinburgh University Press.

Marx, K. ([1859] 1977) *A Contribution to the Critique of Political Economy*. Moscow: Progress Publishers.

McCarty, N., Poole, K. and Rosenthal, H. (2015) *Political Bubbles*. Princeton, NJ: Princeton University Press.

Meijer, A. (2012) The Do It Yourself State. *Information Polity*, *17* (3,4): 303–14. doi: 10.3233/ip-2012-000283.

Meijer, A. (2016) Coproduction as a structural transformation of the public sector. *International Journal of Public Sector Management*, *29* (6): 596–611. doi: 10.1108/ijpsm-01-2016-0001.

Meijer, A. (2018) Datapolis: A public governance perspective on 'Smart Cities'. *Perspectives on Public Management and Governance*, *1* (3): 195–206. E-pub ahead of print doi: 10.1093/ppmgov/gvx017.

Meikle, G. (2014) *Future Active*. New York: Routledge.

Mergel, I., Rethemeyer, R.K. and Isett, K. (2016) Big data in public affairs. *Public Administration Review*, *76* (6): 928–37.

Merica, D. (2017) Clinton to lauch 'resistance' PAC. *CNN politics*, 4 May. Retrieved from https://edition.cnn.com/2017/05/04/politics/clinton-pac-resistance-trump/index.html.

Meynaud, J. (1969) *Technocracy*. New York: Free Press.

Miles, S. (1998) *Consumerism as a Way of Life*. London: Sage.

Miller, C.C. (2008) How Obama's internet campaign changed politics. *New York Times*, 7 November. Retrieved from https://bits.blogs.nytimes.com/2008/11/07/how-obamas-internet-campaign-changed-politics/.

Mintz, S. (1986) *Sweetness and Power*. New York: Penguin Books.

Mirowski, P. (2013) *Never Let a Serious Crisis Go to Waste*. London: Verso.

Mounk, Y. (2018) *The People vs. Democracy: Why Our Freedom Is in Danger and How to Save It*. Cambridge, MA: Harvard University Press.

Mudde, C. (2013) *Are Populists Friends or Foes of Constitutionalism?* Policy Brief, The Social and Political Foundations of Constitutions. The Foundation for Law, Justice and Society, Oxford University. Retrieved from https://ora.ox.ac.uk/objects/uuid:fc657de0-ab0c-4911-8d2b-646101599b65.

Mulgan, G., Tucker, S., Ali, R. and Sanders, B. (2007) *Social Innovation: What it is, Why it Matters and How it can be Accelerated*. Skoll Centre for Social Entrepreneurship. Retrieved from http://eureka.sbs.ox.ac.uk/761/1/Social_Innovation.pdf.

Munro, I. (2017) An interview with Snowden's lawyer: Robert Tibbo on whistle-blowing, mass surveillance and human rights activism. *Organization*, *25* (1): 106–22. doi: 10.1177/1350508417726548.

Nabatchi, T. and Leighninger, M. (2015) *Public Participation for 21st Century Democracy*. Oxford: Wiley.

Nineham, C. (2017) *How the Establishment Lost Control*. Alresford: Zero Books.

O'Neil, C. (2016) *Weapons of Math Destruction*. Harmondsworth: Penguin.

Ospina, S. and Foldy, E. (2015) Enacting collective leadership in a shared-power world. In J. Perry and R. Christensen (eds), *Handbook of Public Administration*. San Francisco, CA: Jossey-Bass.

Peters, B.G. (2016) Governance and the media: Exploring the linkages. *Policy & Politics*, *44* (1): 9–22.

Phillis, J., Deiglmeier, K. and Miller, D. (2008) Rediscovering social innovation. *Stanford Social Innovation Review*, Fall.

Pickard, S. (2017) How Momentum got Britain's youth interested in politics. *LSE Blog*, 5 December.

Pollitt, C. and Bouckaert, G. (2017) *Public Management Reform: A Comparative Analysis Into the Age of Austerity*. Oxford: Oxford University Press.

Porter, M.E. and Kramer, M.R. (2011) The big idea: Creating shared value. *Harvard Business Review*, *89* (1): 2–17.

Postman, N. (2009) *Technopoly*. New York: Random House.

Powell, J. (1996) The multiple self: Exploring between and beyond modernity and postmodernity. *Minnesota Law Review*, *81*.

Reyes (2012) Those Students Again? State-civil society relations during student mobilisations in Chile in 2006 and 2011'. In B. Cannon and P. Kirby (eds) *Civil Society and the State in Left-Led Latin America: Challenges and Limitations to Democratization*. London: Zed Books. pp. 94–111.

Rhodes, R. A. W. (1996) The new governance: Governing without government. *Political studies*, *44*(4): 652–67.

Rhodes, C. and Bloom, P. (2018) The trouble with charitable billionaires. *The Guardian – The Long Read*, 24 May. Retrieved from www.theguardian.com/news/2018/may/24/the-trouble-with-charitable-billionaires-philanthro capitalism.

Roberts, A. (2011) *The Logic of Discipline: Global Capitalism and the Architecture of Government*. Oxford: Oxford University Press.

Roberts, A. (2016) *Four Crises of American Democracy: Representation, Mastery, Discipline, Anticipation*. Oxford: Oxford University Press.

Robertson, R. (1995) Glocalization: Time–space and homogeneity–heterogeneity. *Global Modernities*, *2*: 25–45.

Sanders, B., with Gutman, H. (2015) *An Outsider in the White House*. New York: Verso.

Schumpeter, Joseph A. ([1942] 1950) *Capitalism, Socialism and Democracy*. New York: Harper and Row.

Schwab, K. (2016) *The Fourth Industrial Revolution*. Geneva: World Economic Forum.

Shuster, S. (2016) The Populists. *Time Magazine*, 8 December. Retrieved from http://time.com/time-person-of-the-year-populism/.

Skocpol, T. and Williamson, V. (2016) *The Tea Party and the Remaking of Republican Conservatism*. New York: Oxford University Press.

Smith, D. (2018) 'Trumpwashing': the danger of turning the Republican resistance into liberal heroes. *The Guardian*, 19 September. Retrieved from www.theguardian.com/us-news/2018/sep/19/trumpwashing-republican-resistance-trump-dangers-history.

Smith, J. (2001) Globalizing resistance: The Battle of Seattle and the future of social movements. *Mobilization: An International Quarterly*, *6* (1): 1–19.

Soriano, R. and Nunes, D. (2017) Transforming society as capitalism crumbles: lessons from Brazil's Peasant Movement. *In These Times*, 14 September. Retrieved from http://inthesetimes.com/working/entry/20521/Brazil-MST-Landless-Workers-Peasants-coup-capitalism.

Spicer, A. and Fleming, P. (2007) Intervening in the inevitable: Contesting globalization in a public sector organization. *Organization, 14*(4): 517–41.

Springer, S. (2010). Neoliberal discursive formations: On the contours of subjectivation, good governance, and symbolic violence in posttransitional Cambodia. *Environment and Planning D: Society and Space, 28*(5): 931–50.

Stiglitz, D. (2009) Moving beyond market fundamentalism to a more balanced economy. *Annals of Public and Cooperative Economics, 80* (3): 345–60. doi: 10.1111/j.1467-8292.2009.00389.x.

Taibbi, M. (2013) 'The Secrets and Lies of the Bailout', *Rolling Stone*, 4 January.

Teasdale, S. (2012) What's in a name? Making sense of social enterprise discourses. *Public Policy and Administration, 27*(2): 99–119.

Thomas, J.C. and Streib, G. (2005) E-democracy, E-commerce, and E-research: Examining the electronic ties between citizens and governments. *Administration & Society, 37* (3): 259–80.

Townsend, A.M. (2013) *Smart Cities: Big Data, Civic Hackers, and the Quest for a New Utopia*. New York: WW Norton & Company.

Townshend, J. (2004) Laclau and Mouffe's hegemonic project: The story so far. *Political Studies, 52* (2): 269–88. doi: 10.1111/j.1467-9248.2004.00479.x.

Tsagarousianou, R., Tambini, D. and Bryan, C. (2002) *Cyberdemocracy: Technology, Cities and Civic Networks*. London: Routledge.

Uitermark, J. and Nicholls, W. (2012) How local networks shape a global movement: Comparing Occupy in Amsterdam and Los Angeles. *Social Movement Studies, 11* (3–4): 295–301.

UN-Habitat (2016) *Urbanization and Development: Emerging Futures*. World Cities Report 2016. Nairobi: United Nations Human Settlements Programme.

Vibert, F. (2007) *The Rise of the Unelected: Democracy and the New Separation of Powers*. Cambridge: Cambridge University Press.

Weiler, M. and Pearce, W. (1992) *Reagan and Public Discourse in America (Studies in Rhetoric and Communication)*. Tuscaloosa, AL: University of Alabama Press.

Weiner, L. (2018) Labor renaissance in the heartland. *Jacobin Magazine*, 6 April. Retrieved from https://jacobinmag.com/2018/04/red-state-teachers-strikes-walkouts-unions.

Yates, J. S. and Bakker, K. (2014) Debating the 'post-neoliberal turn' in Latin America. *Progress in Human Geography*, 38(1): 62–90.

Zeleny, M. (2009) Technology and high technology: Support net and barriers to innovation. *Acta Mechanica Slovaca, 13*(1): 6–19.

Žižek, S. (1993) *Tarrying with the Negative*. Durham, NC: Duke University Press.

INDEX